"Our family that spans oceans"

Kakehashi Workbook of Beginning-Intermediate Japanese

Written by: Professor Barrett Balvanz

Illustrated by: Lauren Hostetter

Special Acknowledgements to:

The members of the Sacramento Japanese Meetup

and

my students, past, present and future

Hiragana Chart

Memorize the hiragana alphabet:
(For the full chart, please see page 7 of the textbook.)

あ						か						
い						き						
う						く						
え						け						
お						こ						
が						さ						
ぎ						し						
ぐ						す						
げ						せ						
ご						そ						

た　ち　つ　て　と　な　に　ぬ　ね　の　ば　び　ぶ　べ　ぼ

ざ　じ　ず　ぜ　ぞ　だ　ぢ　づ　で　ど　は　ひ　ふ　へ　ほ

ぱ ぴ ぷ ぺ ぽ や ゆ よ わ ん

ま み む め も ら り る れ ろ を

4

Katakana Chart

Now memorize the katakana alphabet:
(For the full chart, please see page 7 of the textbook.
Also keep in mind that some of the katakana look similar to
or the same as some hiragana.)

ア							カ						
イ							キ						
ウ							ク						
エ							ケ						
オ							コ						
ガ							サ						
ギ							シ						
グ							ス						
ゲ							セ						
ゴ							ソ						

ザ　タ
ジ　チ
ズ　ツ
ゼ　テ
ゾ　ト
ダ　ナ
ヂ　ニ
ヅ　ヌ
デ　ネ
ド　ノ
ハ　バ
ヒ　ビ
フ　ブ
ヘ　ベ
ホ　ボ

パ						マ					
ピ						ミ					
プ						ム					
ペ						メ					
ポ						モ					
ヤ						ラ					
						リ					
ユ						ル					
						レ					
ヨ						ロ					
ワ						ヲ					
ン											

CHAPTER **2** PARTICLES

Writing system true-false quiz

Answer the following statements by writing 'T' if a statement is true and 'F' if it is false.

The Japanese language has 4 writing systems.   ____

Japanese lacked a writing system for most of its history.   ____

There are spaces between words in Japanese writing.   ____

A word can be split across multiple lines of text in Japanese.   ____

Japanese people are very diligent in using punctuation.   ____

Sometimes Japanese people will indent the first line of a new paragraph.   ____

Due to American and European influence, Japanese is no longer written vertically. ____

Japanese is a syllabic language, meaning that every letter is a syllable.   ____

Some letters can be combined with others to make compound syllables.   ____

Subject markers は and が

私（わたし）はやる。 "I will do [something]." vs.

私がやる。 "I will do [something]."

When particle は is used, the speaker is merely denoted as the subject. A basic sentence is formed when the subject is paired with the verb やる meaning "to do." Change the subject particle to が and the extra emphasis placed on the subject (in this case the speaker) adds the nuance of "I –as opposed to anyone else- will do [something]." Say, a group of people are deciding who will do some necessary task –the speaker using particle が would be saying "***I*** will do [the task]."

Try to differentiate between:

これはペンだ。 and これがペンだ。

_____This is a pen._____ vs. _____

彼女（かのじょ）の名前（なまえ）はエミだ。 and 彼女（かのじょ）の名前（なまえ）がエミだ。

____Her name is Emi.____ vs. _____

私（わたし）は運転（うんてん）する。 and 私（わたし）が運転（うんてん）する。

____I will drive.____ vs. _____

妹（いもうと）はケーキを先（さき）に食（た）べた。 and 妹（いもうと）がケーキを先（さき）に食（た）べた。

__My little sister ate cake first__ vs. _____

高橋先生（たかはしせんせい）はとても厳（きび）しい。 and 高橋先生（たかはしせんせい）がとても厳（きび）しい。

Professor Takahashi is super strict. vs. _____

Underline the subject(s) of the following sentences:

これは彼女へのラブレターだ。 "This is a love letter to/for her."

そちらのお方は橋本さんでございます。 (honorific speech) "That person is Mr. Hashimoto."

部屋を出た人はマイケルさんだった。 "The person who left the room was Michael."

日曜日は休みだ。 "Sunday is vacation (my day off)."

毎週の日曜日は休みだ。 "Every week's Sunday is vacation (my day off)."

毎週は日曜日が休みだ。 "Every week, Sunday is vacation (my day off)."

毎週は休みがある。 "Every week [I] have vacation (a day off)."

Fill in the omitted subject along with the appropriate particle:

＿＿うどんを食べる。 "[I] will eat udon."

＿＿金曜日に休みを取る。 "[I] will take vacation (a day off) on Friday."

＿＿寿司を食べたいが、高いから買えないのだ。 "[I] want to eat sushi but, [it] is expensive so I can not buy any."

＿＿＿＿ご飯を食べたか？ "Have [you] eaten food (a meal) [yet]?"

Directional particles に and へ

Draw an arrow to show whether particle に is pointing toward or away from the object then piece together how the sentence would look in English on the line below:

えいがかん　　　　　　い
映画館　　　　に　　行く。
movie theater　　　　go

_____

いえ　　　　　　かえ
家　　　に　帰る。
home　　　return home (verb)

_____

しょくば　　　　　　い
職場　　　へ　　行く　　の。
workplace　　　go　　　?

_____

ひる　はん　　　　　　　　た
昼ご飯　　　に　　カレー　　を　食べた。
lunch　　　　curry　　　　　eat

_____

ともだち
友達　　　に　　プレゼント　　　を　　あげる。
friend　　　present　　　　　　give

_____

かのじょ
彼女　　　に　　　プレゼント　　　を　もらった。
woman/girlfriend　　　present　　　　received

_____

かのじょ
これ　は　彼女　　　から　　もらった　チョコ　だ。
this　woman/girlfriend　received　chocolate　is

_____

11

Underline the subject of the sentence:

わたし　　すうがく　たの
私 には数 学が楽 しいです。 "To me, math is fun."

げつようび　　　かいぎ
月 曜日には会議がある。 "There is a meeting on Monday."

Draw an arrow to show whether へ / から is pointing toward or away from the person, underline the two nouns connected by の then rewrite below how the sentence would look in English:

ともだち
友 達　　　への　　　プレゼント　　　だ。
friend　　　　　present　　　　　　is

_____

ともだち　　　　　　　　てがみ
友 達　　からの　　　手紙 だ。
friend　　　　letter　　　is

_____

Fill in the blank with particle を if the verb is one that acts directly on the object, otherwise write an "X" in the blank space:

かのじょ　　　ま
彼女＿＿待っている。 "[I] am waiting on my girlfriend."

　　　　　た
カレー＿＿食べる。 "[I] will eat curry."

あさ　　じ　がっこう　　　い
朝の7時に学校＿＿行く。 "[I] will go to school at 7 o'clock in the morning."

　　　　　す　　だんせい
チョコ＿＿好きな男性にあげた。 "[I] gave chocolate to the guy I like."

へいじつ　しごと
平日に仕事＿＿する。 "[I] work on weekdays."

　　　　　じ　　じ　　　　はたら
いつも9時から8時まで＿＿働く。 "[I] always work from 9 to 8 o'clock."

あした　ひる　かいぎ
明日は昼から会議＿＿ある。 "Tomorrow, [I] have a meeting from the afternoon on."

ともだち　　　　　　　　　　　　　　　　あ
友達からもらったプレゼント＿＿すぐ開けた。
"[I/he/she] quickly opened the present [I/he/she] had received from a friend."

If you were to ask a question of each of the following people, write in the blank which of the 3 question particles would be most appropriate.

Your immediate supervisor ____

Your immediate supervisor whom you work closely with and know very well ____

Your best friend ____

Your father ____

Your younger sibling ____

A stranger you come across while out and about ____

A much older person sitting next to you on the train ____

Your boss's son who happens to be younger than you ____

Particle の

Use the space provided to the side of the sentence to explain the nature of the relationship between the two nouns connected by particle の **then translate the sentence into English on the line below:**

これ	は	私 (わたし)	の	リュック	です。	_____
this		me		backpack	is	

_____

不幸 (ふこう)	の	手紙 (てがみ)	を	もらった。	_____
unlucky		letter		received	

_____

Add either のか **or** のだ **to the end of each sentence where appropriate.**

Your boss to you: 分かった＿＿＿＿＿？ "Did you get that??"

Explaining yourself to your teacher: 宿題を忘れた＿＿＿＿＿。 "[I] forgot [my] homework."

A coworker asks you: できる＿＿＿＿＿？ "Can [you] do (handle) this?"

You tell an underling: 任せる＿＿＿＿＿。 "[I] delegate this to you."

Your underling replies: 分かりました＿＿＿＿＿。 "[I] understand (and will handle it)."

Particle で

Fill in the blank with the appropriate particle and if it is で **then write in the space to the right whether the particle** で **means "at" or "with" or "by" in that sentence:**

公園 ＿＿	ピックニック	する。	＿＿＿＿＿＿
park	picnic	do (verb)	

来月 ＿＿	引っ越す。		＿＿＿＿＿＿
next month	move house		

自分 ＿＿	やった。		＿＿＿＿＿＿
myself	did		

今年 ＿＿	タバコを	やめる。	＿＿＿＿＿＿
this year	cigarettes	quit	

家 ＿＿	ゆっくり	過ごす。	＿＿＿＿＿＿
house	leisurely	spend time	

車 ＿＿	友達 の	家 に	行った。 ＿＿＿＿＿＿
car	friend	house	went

15

Other uses of Particle と

Fill in the blank with particle と where necessary.

彼 は日本語が 難 しい＿＿言った。　　　　'He said "Japanese is difficult."'

日本語が 難 しい＿＿彼 が言った。　　　　'"Japanese is difficult," he said.'

語学はちょっと 難 しい＿＿思 う。　　　　"[I] think learning languages is a little difficult."

In the following sentences, all of which use との, circle the nouns connected by と and then underline the nouns connected by の, describe the relationship between the nouns denoted by particle の and finally translate the sentence into English.

彼 女 と の　 関 係　 は　 全 く　　　 ない。
Her　　　 relationship　　 absolutely　　 not be/have

＿＿＿＿＿＿＿＿＿＿＿＿＿＿＿＿＿

ジャズ　と　クラシック　との　違 い は　色 々　 ある。
Jazz　　　 classical music　 difference　various　be/have

＿＿＿＿＿＿＿＿＿＿＿＿＿＿＿＿＿

私 と 彼 とのデートはとても 楽 しかった。
I　　 him　 date　　 very　　 awesome/fun　[was]

＿＿＿＿＿＿＿＿＿＿＿＿＿＿＿＿＿

Listing things with Particles と、とか、も **and** や

Construct the following sentences using the words provided and the appropriate particles.

中国の映画＿＿＿日本の映画＿＿＿韓国の映画が好きだ。

"[I] like Chinese, Japanese and Korean movies."

中国の映画＿＿＿韓国の映画＿＿＿が好きだ。

"[I] like Chinese movies, Korean movies and movies from other places."

中国の映画＿＿＿韓国の映画が好きだ。

"[I] like Chinese movies, Korean movies and movies from other places."

中国の映画＿＿＿日本の映画＿＿＿韓国の映画＿＿＿好きだ。

"[I] also like Chinese, Japanese, and Korean movies."

寿司＿＿＿刺身が好きだ。

"[I] like sushi and sashimi and things like that."

ドイツ＿＿＿イタリア＿＿＿フランス＿＿＿スペインに行ったことがある。

"[I] have been to Germany, Italy, France and Spain."

セールだったからシャツ＿＿＿ズボン＿＿＿靴＿＿＿買った。

"Because there was a sale, [I] even bought shirts, pants and shoes!"

Underline and label the subject(s), object(s) and verb(s) in the following sentences then circle and label the particles.

みやもと   ひと
宮本さんはいい人だ。　"Mr/Mrs. Miyamoto is a good person."

きのう   たの   ひ
昨日はとても楽しい日だった。　"Yesterday was a very fun day."

かのじょ　かれ　た   かね　ぜんぶつか
彼女は彼が貯めたお金を全部使った。　"She used all the money he had saved up."

つか　まえ   あら
使う前にフライパンをきれいに洗った。　"[I] washed the fry pan before using it."

にほんご   じゅぎょう   しゅう   さんかいあつ
日本語の授業は週に三回集まる。　"Japanese class gets together 3 times in a (per) week."

かれ　おお   もんだい
彼は大きいな問題がある。　"Regarding him, [a] big problem exists"

わたし　あした　にほんご   しけん
私は明日は日本語の試験がある。　"Regarding myself, as for tomorrow, there is a Japanese test."

Construct a sentence in Japanese using the given words and your knowledge of particles and sentence structure.

today = 今日 is = だ   vacation/day off = 休み

_____

received = もらった present = プレゼント   friend = 友達 I = 私

_____

Next week = 来週   woman/girlfriend = 彼女   date = デート   to do = する

_____

Japanese language = 日本語 class = 授業   like = 好き is = だ

_____

yesterday = 昨日   [was] fun = 楽しかった

_____

I = 私   two [people] = 二人 friend(s) = 友達   present = プレゼント will give = あげる

_____

I = 私   next year = 来年   Japan = 日本   study abroad = 留学する

_____

He = 彼 squid = イカ does not like = 好きじゃない

_____

CHAPTER **4** BASIC CONJUGATION

勝つ (かつ) "to win"

Plain negative _____

Plain past _____

Plain past neg _____

Lesser Polite _____

Polite negative _____

Polite past _____

Polite past neg _____

負ける (まける) "to lose"

Plain negative _____

Plain past _____

Plain past neg _____

Lesser Polite _____

Polite negative _____

Polite past _____

Polite past neg _____

行く (いく) "to go"

Plain negative _____

Plain past _____

Plain past neg _____

Lesser Polite _____

Polite negative _____

Polite past _____

Polite past neg _____

する "to do"

Plain negative _____

Plain past _____

Plain past neg _____

Lesser Polite _____

Polite negative _____

Polite past _____

Polite past neg _____

来る (くる) "to come"

Plain negative _____

Plain past _____

Plain past neg _____

Lesser Polite _____

Polite negative _____

Polite past _____

Polite past neg _____

だ "is"

Plain negative _____

Plain past _____

Plain past neg _____

Lesser Polite _____

Polite negative _____

Polite past _____

Polite past neg _____

いる　"to exist/be located" (sacred things)

Plain negative _____

Plain past _____

Plain past neg _____

Lesser Polite _____

Polite negative _____

Polite past _____

Polite past neg _____

ある　"to exist/be located" (non-sacred things)

Plain negative _____

Plain past _____

Plain past neg _____

Lesser Polite _____

Polite negative _____

Polite past _____

Polite past neg _____

便利 (べんり)　"handy, convenient"

Plain negative _____

Plain past _____

Plain past neg _____

Lesser Polite _____

Polite negative _____

Polite past _____

Polite past neg _____

いい　"good, positive"

Plain negative _____

Plain past _____

Plain past neg _____

Lesser Polite _____

Polite negative _____

Polite past _____

Polite past neg _____

すごい　"wondrous, amazing, incredible"

Plain negative _____

Plain past _____

Plain past neg _____

Lesser Polite _____

Polite negative _____

Polite past _____

Polite past neg _____

はで　"flashy, showy, gaudy"

Plain negative _____

Plain past _____

Plain past neg _____

Lesser Polite _____

Polite negative _____

Polite past _____

Polite past neg _____

Med. Polite	Plain	Meaning	て・Form
します	する	to do	して (non-conforming)
きます	くる	to come	きて (non-conforming)
いきます	いく	to go	いって (non-conforming)
います	いる	to be/exist/be located	
いいます	いう	to say	
のります	のる	to board/get on/ride	
とります	とる	to take/possess/pick up	
あげます	あげる	to give	
くれます	くれる	to receive	
もらいます	もらう	to receive	
しんじます	しんじる	to think/believe	
かちます	かつ	to win	
まけます	まける	to lose	
よみます	よむ	to read	
やります	やる	to do (lower level speech)	
ねます	ねる	to sleep/rest/turn in	
のぼります	のぼる	to climb/hike up	
まがります	まがる	to bend	
かんがえます	かんがえる	to think	
おぼえます	おぼえる	to memorize	
くださいます	くださる	to receive	
おもいます	おもう	to think	
そだちます	そだつ	to raise/grow up	
まなびます	まなぶ	to learn	
しにます	しぬ	to die	
およぎます	およぐ	to swim	
はなします	はなす	to converse	

Descriptor	い or な	Meaning	て form
うつくしい	い	gorgeous	うつくしくて
かんたん	な	simple	かんたんで
はで		gaudy, flashy	
つよい		strong, powerful	
よわい		weak	
あたらしい		new	
ふるい		old	
きれい		pretty, clean	
やさしい		kind	
やすい		cheap	
たかい		high, expensive	
ふくざつ		complex	
きびしい		strict	
はやい		fast	
おそい		slow, late	
へん		strange	
おかしい		strange, funny	
たのしい		enjoyable	
おもしろい		interesting, funny	

Distinguishing between Common Family and Given Names

Write an 'F' next to each family name and a 'G' next to each given name.

まつもと 松本	Pine + true		え み 恵美	Blessed beauty	
いのうえ 井上	Upper well		か ず や 和也	Harmony + to be	
た け だ 武田	Warrior field		の ぶ お 信夫	Faithful man/ husband	
さ と う 佐藤	Junior wisteria		さぶろう 三郎	3rd son	
す ず き 鈴木	Bell tree		しげる 茂	To be luxurious	
なかやま 中山	Middle mountain		たかし 隆	Noble	
しまむら 島村	Island village		つよし 剛	strong	
あい 愛	Love		さいとう 斉藤	Similar wisteria	
あけ み 明美	Bright & beautiful		よし お 義雄	Righteous man	
ち よ 千代	1,000 generations		けん た 健太	Healthy + stout	
けい こ 恵子	Blessed child		けんたろう 健太郎	Healthy, stout son	
やまもと 山本	Mountain + true		かわさき 川崎	River+cape	
こばやし 小林	Small woods		すぎもと 杉本	Cedar + true	
ふ じ 富士	Wealthy retainer		た な か 田中	Middle field	
ないとう 内藤	Inner wisteria		たかはし 高橋	Tall bridge	
ゆ み 由美	Reason & beauty		ようこ 陽子	Sun child	

Given each prompt, write the appropriate suffix after each name or title.

(Talking to your superior, Division Manager Yamada)　　部長＿＿＿

(Talking *about* Division Manager Yamada)　　山田部長＿＿＿

(Talking to another section's manager, Iguchi)　　井口課長＿＿＿

(Talking to one's own section manager)　　課長＿＿＿

(Addressing your neighbor, Mrs. Watanabe)　　渡辺＿＿＿

(Talking *about* your neighbor, Mrs. Watanabe)　　渡辺＿＿＿

(Talking to a client, Mr. Yoshimoto)　　吉本＿＿＿

(Talking *about* a client, Mr. Yoshimoto)　　吉本＿＿＿

(Addressing your own son, Yoshihiro)　　よしひろ＿＿＿

(Addressing your own daughter, Aki)　　あき＿＿＿

Given each scenario, write 'Y' if it is ok to use a personal pronoun or 'N' if it is not.

(A married woman addresses her husband by あなた)　　＿＿＿

(A married man addresses his wife by あなた)　　＿＿＿

(A man addresses his girlfriend by きみ)　　＿＿＿

(A woman refers to herself by あたし)　　＿＿＿

(A boss addresses an underling by おまえ)　　＿＿＿

Fill in the blanks with the appropriate demonstrative pronouns.

this book ＿＿の本   that book ＿＿の本   that one book ＿＿の本   which book ＿＿の本

this book ＿＿本   that book ＿＿本   that one book ＿＿本   which book ＿＿本

this kind of book ＿＿本   that kind of book ＿＿本   that one kind of book ＿＿本

which kind of book ＿＿本

here ＿＿   there ＿＿   that one place ＿＿ where ＿＿

this here book ＿＿の本   that there book ＿＿の本   the book at that one place ＿＿の本

the book at where ＿＿の本

Write the proper reply next to each greeting.

When meeting (not for the first time)

こんにちは〜   ＿＿＿＿＿＿＿＿＿＿＿＿＿＿＿＿＿＿＿＿＿

おはよう〜   ＿＿＿＿＿＿＿＿＿＿＿＿＿＿＿＿＿＿＿＿＿

今晩は〜   ＿＿＿＿＿＿＿＿＿＿＿＿＿＿＿＿＿＿＿＿＿

おはようございます。   ＿＿＿＿＿＿＿＿＿＿＿＿＿＿＿＿＿＿＿＿＿

Your boss says おはよう   ＿＿＿＿＿＿＿＿＿＿＿＿＿＿＿＿＿＿＿＿＿

久しぶりです。(it's been a while)   ＿＿＿＿＿＿＿＿＿＿＿＿＿＿＿＿＿＿＿＿＿

久しぶり〜！   ＿＿＿＿＿＿＿＿＿＿＿＿＿＿＿＿＿＿＿＿＿

When parting ways:

では〜 _____

じゃあね〜！ _____

じゃあ〜 _____

失礼します。 _____
しつれい

またね。 _____

是非また会いましょう！(Let's definitely meet up again!) _____
ぜひ   あ

Write the name or title that you should address the following people by making sure to add any necessary prefixes or suffixes.

Your supervisor who is named 杉本あやこ _____
                              すぎもと

The section manager (課長) named 中島のりお _____
                      かちょう   なかじま

Your friend 高橋さちこ _____
           たかはし

A young boy (given name is 誠) _____
                          まこと

A young girl (given name is 夏子) _____
                           なつこ

Fill in the blank with the appropriate word(s) of thanks given the prompt.

(to a friend who has shared some gum with you) _____

(to a waiter in a restaurant) _____

(to someone who has just saved your child's life) _____

(to a coworker who has brought you a souvenir) _____

(to your host who has cooked a meal for you) _____

Fill in the blank with the appropriate word(s) of apology given the prompt.

(to your boss when leaving his office) _____

(to someone you bump into on a crowded street) _____

(to someone accidentally tripped) _____

(to a customer whose order you mixed up) _____

(to a friend who has had to listen to you complain) _____

Given the prompt, write in the blank whether you think the person replying replied in the affirmative, refused consent, or merely signaled that he/she was paying attention.

Boss: 来年までに売り上げを倍にしよう。 "[I] want to double sales by next year."

Employee: はい。 _____

Friend: 言っていることを聞いているの。 "Are [you] listening to what [I'm] saying?"

You: はい。 _____

Mother: 今年に昇進すると聞いた。 "[I] heard you will be promoted this year."

Son: ええ。 _____

Wife: 6時ごろに帰るの。 "Will [you] return home around 6pm?"

Husband: いいえ、8時ごろだ。 _____ around 8pm.

Host: お代わりを食べますか。 "Will [you] have (eat) seconds?"

Guest: いいですよ。 _____

Supervisor: レポートは金曜日までにできる？ "Can [you] do (finish) the report by Friday?"

You: それはちょっと。。。 _____

Introductions

Convert the plain speech introductions into honorific speech.

これは金田_{かねだ}さんだ。 _____

この人は池田_{いけだ}さんだ。 _____

宮本_{みやもと}だ。 _____

よろしく。 _____

はじめまして〜 (宮本_{みやもと}だ。) _____

(introducing your boss)これは山本課長_{やまもとかちょう}だ。 _____

Write the following numbers in kanji below then write the pronunciation in hiragana.

127   43,689   2,540,863

_____   _____   _____

_____   _____   _____

Write the following amounts in kanji then write the pronunciation in hiragana.

4 DVDs   3 pencils   2 cars

_____   _____   _____

_____   _____   _____

10 times (occasions)   14 people   1 house

_____   _____   _____

_____   _____   _____

27 floors   2,400 yen   5 little trinkets

_____   _____   _____

_____   _____   _____

Write the following times in kanji and then write the pronunciation in hiragana.

5:30 am   18:00   11 o'clock

_____   _____   _____

_____   _____   _____

Write the following amounts of time in kanji and then write the pronunciation in hiragana.

2 years   1 week   Hour and a half

_____   _____   _____

_____   _____   _____

35 minutes   3 months   4 hours

_____   _____   _____

_____   _____   _____

1 day   An entire day   6 days

_____   _____   _____

_____   _____   _____

Write the following dates in kanji and then write the pronunciation below.

November 2nd 2011   2/12/1993   August the sixth 1981

_____   _____   _____

_____   _____   _____

12/25/1901   01/01/2000   9/20/1999

_____   _____   _____

_____   _____   _____

March 20th 1986   June 10, 1991   5/5/2005

_____   _____   _____

_____   _____   _____

CHAPTER 7 IN THE HOME

第
課

Verb in て form + いる・います

Verb (plain)	Lesser-polite	う,る or irregular?	Plain speech て+いる	Lesser-polite て+います
はなす	はなします			
いく	いきます			
あるく	あるきます			
およぐ	およぎます			
はしる	はしります			
のむ	のみます			
たべる	たべます			
あげる	あげます			
よむ	よみます			
おぼえる	おぼえます			
そだつ	そだちます			
まける	まけます			
かつ	かちます			
あわせる	あわせます			
しんじる	しんじます			
ねる	ねます			
なる	なります			
かんがえる	かんがえます			
あう	あいます			
しぬ	しにます			
よぶ	よびます			
くる	きます			

から

Write 'F' in the blank if the から in the sentence means "from" and 'B' if it means "because/so."

駅 から 家 までは2キロ だ。 ___
Station [my] house 2 kilometers is

お腹 が 空いた から 食べよう。 ___
Stomach empty let's eat

好き だ から また 買う と 思う。 ___
Like is again buy [I] think

すし は 高い から 買えない。 ___
Sushi high (expensive) can't buy

友達 から の 手紙 だ。 ___
Friend letter is

それ から まっすぐ 歩いたら、 10分 かかる。 ___
(there) straight if walk 10 minutes will take

が・けど

Fill in the blank with either が or けど to complete the sentence.

友達の家を訪ねた _____ 友達は いなかった。
[I] visited a friend's house but [my] friend was not home.

トマトが好きだ _____ トマトスープが好きじゃない。
[I] like tomatoes but [I] do not like tomato soup.

職場に行く _____ 早めに帰る。
[I] will go to the office but [I] will return home early.

彼女と話してみた _____ 別れた。
[I] tried talking with her (my girlfriend) but we broke up.

て + ください

Read the translations and then conjugate the verbs in the Japanese sentences into commands (て form) and add ください to change the level of speech where necessary.

Your boss says to you: "Come here for a second."

ちょっとこっちに来る => ちょっとこっちに来＿＿＿＿＿＿＿＿＿

You say to your supervisor: "Listen to this for a second."

これをちょっと聞く => これをちょっと聞＿＿＿＿＿＿＿＿

Your supervisor says to his/her boss: "Read this report."

このレポートを読む => このレポートを読＿＿＿＿＿＿＿＿

You say to your girlfriend: "take out the trash."

ごみを出す => ごみを出＿＿＿＿＿＿＿＿

Addressing and Speaking about Family

Fill in the chart below making sure the add prefixes and suffixes where necessary.

	talking about your family		talking about someone else's family	
	to a family member	to someone else	to that person directly	to someone else
little brother				
little sister				
older brother				
older sister				
Mother				
Father				
parent's younger brother				
parent's younger sister				
parent's older brother				
parent's older sister				
Grandmother				
Grandfather				
Wife				
Husband				

Set phrases used when leaving and returning

For each of the following situations, write the appropriate phrase in the appropriate level of speech.

Leaving the home you share with your wife   _____

Leaving your parent's home   _____

Leaving the office to go to a meeting   _____

Returning home from work   _____

Returning to the office from a meeting   _____

When your wife returns home   _____

When your husband returns home   _____

When your colleague returns from a business trip   _____

When your husband leaves the house   _____

When your wife leaves the house   _____

Practice with Colors and Prepositions

Take a look at a mockup of what the living room in the above apartment might look like.

Noting the colors and relative locations of the objects fill in the blanks to complete the sentences below which describe objects in the room.

＿＿＿＿＿ソファ は リビング の 真ん中 に ある。
    Sofa living room center exists/be/is located

テレビ が テレビ台 の＿＿＿＿＿ に ある。
 TV   TV stand   exists/be/is located

ドアの＿＿＿＿＿に 本棚 が ある。
Door   bookshelf exists/be/is located

本棚 の＿＿＿＿＿にテーブル と いす が ある。
Bookshelf   table and chairs exists/be/are located

色々な＿＿＿＿＿の 本 が ある。
Various   books exist/be/are located

テレビ台 の 横 に＿＿＿＿＿ 色 の 植木鉢 が ある。
TV stand next to   color pot exists/be/is located

＿＿＿＿＿ 色 の 植木鉢に 植物 が 植えてある。
    color pot   plant is planted

その 植物 は＿＿＿＿＿色の葉っぱ が ある。
that plant   color leaves exists/has

二つの＿＿＿＿＿ いす が ある。
 two   chairs exist/be/are located

＿＿＿＿＿手 の 壁 に 時計 が 掛かってある。
hand [side] wall clock is hanging

一	イチ、イッ　ひと　one												
二	ニ　ふた　two												
三	サン　み　three												
四	シ　よ、よん　four												
五	ゴ　いつ　five												
六	ロク　む、むい　six												
七	シチ　なな、なの　seven												
八	ハチ、ハッ　や　eight												
九	キュウ、ク　ここの　nine												
十	ジュウ　とお　ten												
百	ヒャク、ビャク、ピャク　hundred												
千	セン、ゼン　thousand												
万	マン、バン　ten thousand, infinite												

行	コウ、ギョウ go, behavior　いく "to go"　おこなう "to carry out, put on an event"									
来	ライ　くる "to come"									
日	ヒ、ビ　にち、に、じつ day, sun, Japan									
月	ゲツ、ガツ　month, moon, flesh　つき moon									
火	カ　ひ、ほ fire, flame									
水	スイ　みず water									
木	モク　き tree, wood, wooden									
金	キン、コン　money, gold かね money									
土	ト、ド　land, area, plot つち dirt									
年	ネン　とし year									
時	ジ　time, counter for hours　とき time									
分	フン、ブン、プン　わかる to analyze and understand　わける to break down　わかれる be broken down									

CHAPTER 8 TRANSPORTATION

Deriving meaning from context with どのぐらい and かかる

Given the following prompts write in the blank what the speaker would be referring to if he/she were to ask どのぐらいかかる？

When asking a station manager about ticket price _____

When in a rush and asking how many times the train will stop _____

When asking directions at a コンビに _____

When asking your instructor about mastering Japanese _____

Dissecting Japanese Addresses

しずおかけんしずおかしするがくつしまちょう　ちょうめ
静岡県静岡市駿河区津島町3丁目2-3-405

_____

あいちけんなごやしひがしくやまぐちちょう　　ちょうめ
愛知県名古屋市東区山口町2丁目4-1-216

_____

Fill in 番 to complete the following dialogs.

A:　山口市に行きたいですが、何＿＿＿バスですか。
"[I] want to go to Yamaguchi, but what bus is it (should I take)?"

B:　１３８＿＿＿バスですよ。　"It is (you should take) the #138 bus."

A:　＿＿＿＿＿＿＿＿好きなアニメのキャラクターは誰ですか。"What is [your] favorite anime character?"

B:　＿＿＿＿＿＿＿＿好きなキャラクターは「ルパン」ですよ。"[My] favorite character is Lupin III."

Now try your hand at replying to questions like the above by responding using the same structure (or at least the same verb) as the original question.

朝に何時に起きる？　"What time do [you] wake up in the morning?"

＿＿＿＿＿＿＿＿＿＿＿＿＿＿＿＿＿＿＿＿＿＿＿。　"[I] wake up at 8'oclock in the morning."

アニメと漫画とどれが好きですか。　"Which do you like [better] anime or manga?"

＿＿＿＿＿＿＿＿＿＿＿＿＿＿＿＿＿＿＿＿＿＿＿。　"[I] like manga."

昼食に中華料理をまた食べますか。　"Will you eat Chinese food for lunch again?"

＿＿＿＿＿＿＿＿＿＿＿＿＿＿＿＿＿＿＿＿＿＿＿。　"No, [I] will eat sushi."

この電車は山口駅で止ますか。　"Will this train stop at Yamaguchi station?"

＿＿＿＿＿＿＿＿＿＿＿＿＿＿＿＿＿＿＿＿＿＿＿。　"[It] will stop at Yamaguchi station."

どうやって、どうして、どうした

Complete the following sentences by adding one of the above compounds.

_____カレーを作^{つく}る？
　　　　　　　Curry　　make

_____の？痛^{いた}そうだ。
　　　　　　　　[That] looks like [it] hurts.

_____ここにいるの？
　　　　　　　Here　be

_____この電車^{でんしゃ}が 小倉駅^{こくらえき} で 止^とまらなかった？
　　　　　　　This　　train　　Kokura Station not stop

_____か、分^わからない。
　　　　　　　　I don't know.

_____日本語^{にほんご}を より　　速^{はや}く　　学^{まな}べるか。
　　　　　　Japanese language　more so　quickly　able to learn

Sorting out いい vs. よい

Consult the following chart and then fill in the appropriate conjugation to complete the sentences below.

		Positive	Negative
Future	Plain	いい・よい	
	L. Polite		
Past	Plain		
	L. Polite		

Between friends: ね、あの映画^{えいが}は_____ (wasn't good)。

To your supervisor: このレポートは_____(well)分^わかりません。

Softening a Statement with 思う

Add と思う to the end of only the statements that you feel need softening.

すしが好<ruby>好<rt>す</rt></ruby>きだ＿＿＿＿＿＿＿。"[I] like sushi."

すしは<ruby>最<rt>もっと</rt></ruby>も<ruby>美味<rt>おい</rt></ruby>しい<ruby>食<rt>た</rt></ruby>べ<ruby>物<rt>もの</rt></ruby>だ＿＿＿＿＿＿＿。"[I] think sushi is the most delicious food."

Everyone else: ラーメンがいいよね。"Ramen is great eh??"

You: すし<ruby>好<rt>す</rt></ruby>きがいい＿＿＿＿＿＿＿。"[I] think sushi is good."

これは<ruby>間違<rt>まちが</rt></ruby>った＿＿＿＿＿＿＿。"This is incorrect / mistaken."

車	シャ　くるま　wheel, axel, car										
乗	ジョウ　のる　ride, board, pilot										
降	コウ　ふる　fall (rain etc.)　おりる　disembark　おろす　let/make disembark										
曲	キョク　counter for songs　まげる　to ben, turn something　まがる　to be bended, to turn										
進	シン　すすむ　to progress, continue, advance										
止	シ　とめる　to stop something　とまる　to stop										
取	シュ　とる　to take										
歩	ホ　あるく　to walk										
走	ソウ　はしる　to run										
道	ドウ　みち　road, path, way, way of doing										
町	チョウ　まち　town, neighborhood										
街	ガイ　まち　town, street, district										
駅	えき　station										

本	ほん book, counter for long and/or cylindrical objects											
円	エン Japanese currency　まる circle　まるい round, circular											
人	ニン、ジン person/people, counter for people　ひと person/people											
上	ジョウ　うえ up, above, on top　あげる raise　あがる rise											
下	カ、ゲ　した down, below　さげる bring down　さがる lower, go down											
左	サ　ひだり left											
右	ユウ　みぎ right											
中	チュウ、ジュウ　なか middle, inside, inbetween											
外	ガイ　そと outside, other											
答	トウ　こたえる to reply, respond, answer											
多	タ　おおい many											
少	ショウ　すくない few											

Complete the sentence by adding either に来る or に行く to the stem of the verb.

EX: 山を登る<u>りに行く</u>　　　。 "[I] will go to climb [the] mountain."

友達とすしを食べる_____。 "[I] will go with a friend to eat sushi."

ニューヨークまで彼女を会う_____。
"[I] will go as far as New York to meet with [my] girlfriend."

東アジアの歴史を勉強する_____。 "[I] have come to study East Asian history."

地震を調べる_____。 "[I] have come to investigate (research) the earthquake."

Expressing desire with 欲しい

Conjugate the verb into て form and then add ほしい to turn the sentence into a request.

Ex: 宿題を<u>するしてほしい</u>　　　。 "[I] want [you] to do [your] homework."

晩ご飯を全部食べる_____。 "[I] want [you] to eat all of [your] dinner."

部屋を片付け<u>る</u>_____。 "[I] want [you] to clean [your] room."

この雑誌を見<u>る</u>_____。 "[I] want [you] to take a look at this magazine."

速く着替え<u>る</u>_____。 "[I] want [you] to quickly get changed."

このレポートを読<u>む</u>_____。 "[I] want [you] to read this report."

Fill in the appropriate compound word (noun + でも) to complete the sentence.

_____できないというのか。
Are you saying that you can't do *even that!?*

好きなものは_____あげるから 教えてください。
[I] will give you anything you want, so teach (tell) [me what it is].

このドアを開けてくれたら_____いいのよ。
If [he/she] opens this door, whomever is fine!!

_____いいけどレポートを金曜日までに終わらせなさい。
However is fine, but finish [the] report by Friday!

Fill in the blank of the sentence with the appropriate conjugation of いい "good."

_____席を予約しました。 "[I] reserved good seats."

奥様の具合が_____。 "[Your] wife's health is not good."

彼の日本語の 能 力は_____が、上手くなった。
His knowledge of Japanese was not good, but he has become skillful.

Fill in the blank to complete the sentence with the appropriate verb.

言う　　To say　　考える　　To think (cognize)

喋る　　To speak　　思う　　To think/feel

話す　　To converse

お客さんが英語が分からないから日本語で＿＿＿＿＿＿＿。
The client does not understand English so please speak in Japanese.

うちの提案を＿＿＿＿＿＿＿。
Please think about [my] proposal.

あの人たちと＿＿＿＿＿＿＿悪い人だと＿＿＿＿＿＿＿。
[I] talked to those people and [I] don't think [they] are bad people.

彼はうちの提案についてなんと＿＿＿＿＿＿＿？
What did he say about my proposal?

彼女がそれを＿＿＿＿＿＿ことが本当だと＿＿＿＿＿＿＿か。
[Do you] think that it is true that she said that?

＿＿＿＿＿＿＿上で、提案を断ります。
Having thought about it, [I] refuse [to adopt] the proposal.

Fill in the blank with either 前 or 後 as appropriate.

皿 を 汚す_____きれいに 洗って。
Dishes   dirty (v)   wash [them] (until they shine)

食べる_____皿 を ちゃんと あらって。
 Eat   dishes   fully   wash [them]

家 を 全部 掃除した_____お風呂に 入った。
House   all of   clean   bath   get in

麺 を 入れる_____お湯 を 沸かす。
Noodles   put in   hot water   boil

学	ガク the study of- まなぶ to learn												
校	コウ institution												
小	コ、ショウ small, lessor ちいさい small												
高	コウ たかい high, tall												
公	コウ public												
私	シ private わたし、わたくし I, me												
立	リツ たつ to stand												
先	セン さき immediately in front of oneself												
生	セイ、ショウ なま live いきる to live うむ to birth												
教	キョウ education おしえる to teach												
室	シツ room												
大	ダイ、タイ large, great, grand おおきい large												
入	ニュウ enter はいる to enter いれる to put in いる to be in												

出	シュツ exit, leave　だす to take out, bring out, shoot out　でる to exit, come out									
北	ホク　きた North									
南	ナン　みなみ South									
東	トウ　ひがし East									
西	サイ、セイ　にし West									
子	シ　こ child									
語	ゴ language　かたる to tell a story									
英	エイ England, noble									
国	コク　くに country, nation									
正	セイ、ショウ　ただしい correct, just, proper									
別	ベツ separate　わかれる to separate									
門	モン gate									

欲しい vs. たい
(ほ)

Conjugate the following verbs into both たい and ほしい forms and then translate the meaning.

飲む "to drink" (の)　　　_____たい　　　_____

　　　　　　　　　　　　_____ほしい　　_____

知る "to know" (し)　　　_____たい　　　_____

　　　　　　　　　　　　_____ほしい　　_____

運転する "to drive" (うんてん)　_____たい　　　_____

　　　　　　　　　　　　_____ほしい　　_____

買う "to buy" (か)　　　　_____たい　　　_____

　　　　　　　　　　　　_____ほしい　　_____

任せる "to delegate" (まか)　_____たい　　　_____

　　　　　　　　　　　　_____ほしい　　_____

Ways to express hunger

For each situation, write how you should express your hunger.

When talking to your friend　　_____

When talking to your coworker　_____

When talking to your younger sibling　_____

When talking to your parent　_____

Expressing "Let's" or "shall we?"

Verb (plain)	Lesser-polite	う,る or irregular?	Verb stem	Plain speech よう	Lesser-polite ましょう
はなす	はなします				
いく	いきます				
あるく	あるきます				
およぐ	およぎます				
はしる	はしります				
のむ	のみます				
たべる	たべます				
あげる	あげます				
よむ	よみます				
おぼえる	おぼえます				
そだつ	そだちます				
まける	まけます				
かつ	かちます				
ねる	ねます				
なる	なります				
あわせる	あわせます				
あう	あいます				
しんじる	しんじます				
かんがえる	かんがえます				
くる	きます				
しぬ	しにます				
よぶ	よびます				
する	します				
あそぶ	あそびます				
いう	いいます				
いる	います				
うまれる	うまれます				
おく	おきます				
かりる	かります				
きる	きります				
ふる	ふります				

Conditional Form with ～えば

Verb (plain)	Lesser-polite	う,る or irregular?	Verb stem	えば (conditional form)
はなす	はなします			
いく	いきます			
あるく	あるきます			
およぐ	およぎます			
はしる	はしります			
のむ	のみます			
たべる	たべます			
あげる	あげます			
よむ	よみます			
おぼえる	おぼえます			
そだつ	そだちます			
まける	まけます			
かつ	かちます			
ねる	ねます			
なる	なります			
あわせる	あわせます			
あう	あいます			
しんじる	しんじます			
かんがえる	かんがえます			
くる	きます			
しぬ	しにます			
よぶ	よびます			
する	します			
あそぶ	あそびます			
いう	いいます			
いる	います			
うまれる	うまれます			
おく	おきます			
かりる	かります			
きる	きります			
ふる	ふります			

Noun + に + する

Pick nouns from the box and write them along with にする on the lines below. Only some of the nouns logically work with にする so choose carefully.

最高 "best"　無駄 "a waste"　すし　ケーキ "cake"　食べ "eat"　注文 "order"

デザート "dessert"　最後 "last"　賭け "a bet"　好き "as one likes"　ジュース "juice"

1. _____

2. _____

3. _____

4. _____

5. _____

6. _____

7. _____

Have you ever...?　ことがある？

Using the words provided, complete the following sentences while adding ことがある and then make the sentences into questions. Keep in mind that the action verb must be conjugated into the past tense.

メキシコに行く "go to Mexico"

_____?

刺身を食べる "eat raw food"

_____?

歌を歌う "sing a song"

_____?

うわさをする "spread a rumor"

_____?

Now pretend that someone has asked you the above questions. Using the same grammar structure, answer the questions on the lines below.

_____?

_____?

_____?

_____?

Noun + に + Verb

Pick the noun from the box that correctly completes the sentence and write it in the blank.

飲み "drinking"　　返し "return"　　遊び "playing"　　すし

きれい "pretty/clean"　　話し "conversation"　　スキーをし "skiing"　　パン "bread"

パン生地 を オーブンで 焼けば＿＿＿＿＿になる。
Bread dough   oven   if bake

仕事の後に友達と＿＿＿＿＿に行く。
Work after friend(s)

友達 は 家に＿＿＿＿＿に来る。
Friend house

ヨーロッパの 最も 高い 山　まで　　＿＿＿＿＿に行った。
Europe   most   tall mountain until (all the way for)

この 魚 は＿＿＿＿＿になる。
This fish

お風呂に入れば＿＿＿＿＿になる。
Bath   if enter

後　少しに 彼女 が ＿＿＿＿＿に来る。
Later little in/at she/girlfriend

ビデオ を ＿＿＿＿＿に行く。
rental movie

食	ショク　たべる　to eat										
飲	イン　のむ　to drink										
飯	ハン　めし　cooked rice, a meal										
米	マイ、メ　こめ　rice, America										
和	ワ　harmony, Japan, Japanese										
屋	オク　や　roof, house, shop, dealer										
料	リョウ　fee, materials										
理	リ　logic, arrangement, reason										
魚	ギョウ　さかな　fish										
肉	ニク　flesh/ meat										
物	ブツ　もの　a physical (tangible) thing										
注	チュウ　そそぐ、つぐ　to flow, to pour										
文	ブン、モン　sentence, literature, art										

待	タイ　まつ　to wait										
好	コウ　すき　like, love　このむ　to prefer										
今	コン　いま　now										
会	カイ　あう　to meet										
家	カ　いえ　house, home, family										
回	カイ　counter for # of repetitions,　まわる　to revolve										
計	ケイ　はかる　plot, scheme, to measure										
海	カイ　うみ　ocean										
酒	シュ　さけ　alcohol										
氷	ヒョウ　こおり　ice,　こおる　to freeze										
刀	トウ　blade　かたな　sword, medium length sword　そり　razor										
田	デン　た　field, rice paddy										

CHAPTER **11** SHOPPING
第課

Asking & Giving Permission

Write sentences in 日本語（にほんご） asking permission to do the following things:

May I go beforehand?

May I return home at 6pm?

May I turn in my homework a little late? (turn in = 出（だ）す)

May I ask you a question?

Now translate these responses into 日本語（にほんご）:

You may not go to the bathroom right now.

You may begin the test.

You may leave work early on Thursday.

You may not leave until the test period is over.

I guess I'll... ～ようかなと<ruby>思<rt>おも</rt></ruby>う

Write the following in <ruby>日本語<rt>にほんご</rt></ruby>:

I have been thinking of dieting. (diet[ing] = ダイエットする)

Takashi was thinking of going to the ocean. (ocean = <ruby>海<rt>うみ</rt></ruby>)

I have been thinking of studying together with my friend.

I have been thinking of going to visit my folks. (visit family = <ruby>実家<rt>じっか</rt></ruby>に<ruby>帰<rt>かえ</rt></ruby>る)

Give it a try with てみる

Write the following in <ruby>日本語<rt>にほんご</rt></ruby>:

I will try studying more.

I will try eating nattou.

I will try walking (and going) to the office. (office = <ruby>職場<rt>しょくば</rt></ruby>)

I will try to have a talk with him.

ので・のに

Write the following in 日本語(にほんご):

I did not study so I did not pass the test.

She forgot her homework so the professor got mad. (get mad = 怒(おこ)る)

Today I feel (am) happy/energetic so I want to have fun! (want to have fun = 遊(あそ)びたいんだ)

Tomorrow I will be busy so I can't do anything.

Even though it is pretty, I do not like it.

Let's wait a little longer even though he is late.

Even though I read a lot, I still don't understand it.

Even though he is not famous, I still like him.

Able-to Form with ～える

Verb (plain)	Lesser-polite	う,る or irregular?	Able-to form	Stem of the able-to form
はなす	はなします			
いく	いきます			
あるく	あるきます			
およぐ	およぎます			
はしる	はしります			
のむ	のみます			
たべる	たべます			
あげる	あげます			
よむ	よみます			
おぼえる	おぼえます			
そだつ	そだちます			
まける	まけます			
かつ	かちます			
ねる	ねます			
なる	なります			
あわせる	あわせます			
あう	あいます			
しんじる	しんじます			
かんがえる	かんがえます			
くる	きます			
しぬ	しにます			
よぶ	よびます			
する	します			
あそぶ	あそびます			
いう	いいます			
いる	います			
うまれる	うまれます			
おく	おきます			
かりる	かります			
きる	きります			
ふる	ふります			

Expressing ability with ことができる

Taking into account the given situation, write the underlined parts in 日本語 (にほんご). Depending on the situation you may need to conjugate the verb into える or ことができる.

After a bicyclist was hit by a car, a bystander asks "Can you walk?"

One's host at a business meeting asks "Can you drink sake?"

After accidentally knocking over an antique in a shop you reassure the owner "I can pay."

Responding to a nurse's questions, you say "I can eat."

A blind person might say "I can read with my fingers."

A coworker asks if you can read Japanese.

An Olympic contender might boast that he can run really fast.

A person in a wheelchair would say that she cannot run.

Verb stem+にくい・やすい

Translate the following sentences into 日本語:

Kanji are very difficult to memorize. (memorize = 覚える)

It is easy to make new friends at school. (make a friend = 友達を作る)

My friend is very skillful so it is difficult to beat him at chess. (skillful = 上手 beat=win=勝つ)

It is not easy to raise a child. (raise = 育てる)

Old English is very difficult to read. (old = 昔の)

She is very smart so it is easy to believe her. (smart = 頭がいい)

It is a steep trail so it is easy to fall and get hurt. (steep trail = 急な登り道 fall = 落ちる
get hurt = 怪我をする)

It is difficult to get used to a new job. (get used to = 慣れる)

Connecting descriptors to verbs with く・に

Descriptor	Verb	Compound	Meaning
忙しい （いそが）	なる		
駄目 （だめ）	する		
		速く帰る （はや　かえ）	
		完全に終わらせる （かんぜん　お）	
嫌い （きら）	なる		(be)come to hate (something)
		完璧にできる （かんぺき）	can do something perfectly
バラバラ	切る （き）		cut haphazardly into lots of pieces
遅い （おそ）	寝る （ね）		
深い （ふか）	感じる （かん）		feel deeply
静か （しず）	話す （はな）		
よい	ある		
永い （なが）	走る （はし）		

比	ヒ comparative/contrasting くらべる to compare											
品	ヒン しな good(s), item(s)											
買	バイ かう to buy											
売	バイ うる to sell											
店	テン みせ store, shop											
色	ショク color いろ color, sex											
借	シャク debt かりる to borrow											
貸	タイ かす to lend											
返	ヘン かえる to return かえす to return something											
付	フ つく be attached つける to attach											
見	ケン みる to see/look/watch みえる to be able to see みせる to show											
安	アン calm, safe, peace やすい cheap											
長	チョウ boss, main ながい long											

員	イン　member										
価	カ　value										
客	キャク、カク　guest, client, customer										
銀	ギン　silver										
商	ショウ　trade, commerce										
市	シ　City　いち　market										
場	ジョウ　ば　place										
所	ショ　place　ところ　point										
持	ジ　もつ　to have, hold, possess, own										
着	チャク　wear, counter for clothing　つく　to arrive　きる　to wear										
洋	ヨウ　foreign, American/European										
服	フク　clothing										

CHAPTER 12 MEDICAL CARE IN JAPAN

第
課

Changing sentence structure with だから・からだ

Fill in the blank with either だから or からだ and keep the level of speech in mind.

明日はクイズの日＿＿＿＿＿＿ 勉 強 する。
"[It] is because tomorrow is the day of the quiz that I will study."

(said to a different professor) 明日に日本語のクイズがある＿＿＿＿＿＿。
"[It] is because [I] have a quiz tomorrow."

(said to the doctor) お腹がすごく痛い＿＿＿＿＿＿。
[It] is because my stomach really hurts."

(said to a friend) 暇＿＿＿＿＿＿手伝うよ。
"[It] is because [I am] totally free that [I] will help you."

Making observations with よう,そう & らしい

Fill in the blank with the appropriate ending and then explain why that ending works.

結構 稼いでいる_____。 ”[It] seems that [you] have been really raking in the money.”
(けっこうかせ)

_____

ビジネスがうまく行っている_____。 ”[It] seems that business (must be) going well.”
(い)

_____

来 年から飛行機のチケットが 高くなる_____。 ”[It] seems that plane tickets will become
(らいねん)(ひこうき)(たか)   more expensive from next year on.”

_____

彼 のこのスマートフォンは便利_____。 ”[It] seems that his smartphone is (very) handy.”
(かれ)(べんり)

_____

この豆腐が 腐っている_____。 “[It] seems that this tofu is rotten/spoiled.”
(とうふ)(くさ)

_____

今度の 先 生は男 性_____。 “[It] seems that our next professor is a guy.”
(こんど)(せんせい)(だんせい)

_____

あの女 優は海 外でも有 名_____。 “[It] seems that that actress is famous even overseas.”
(じょゆう)(かいがい)(ゆうめい)

_____

73

Rewrite the below sentences using the given grammar point and level of speech.

田中さんはサッカー部を辞める。 "Tanaka will quit the Soccer team."
(Use そう) (Speaking to a classmate)

_____

山田さんの車はまた壊れた。 "Yamada's car has broken down again!"
(Use よう) (Said by a mechanic teasing a repeat customer)

_____

あのアプリがとても役に立つ。 "That app really comes in handy!"
(Use らしい) (Said by a friend recommending another friend to download an app)

_____

そのデパートにある店は高い。 "The shops in that department store are expensive."
(Use らしい) (Said by a coworker cautioning another coworker)

_____

あの歌手はメキシコ人だ。 "That singer is of Mexican nationality."
(Use よう) (Speaking to a friend)

_____

あのレストランの店内はとても派手だ。 "That restaurant's interior is very flashy/wild."
(Use そう) (Said by an underling relating his observation to his boss, the owner of a competing restaurant)

_____

また, まだ & まだまだ

Fill in the blanks with one of the above three words to complete the sentence.

_____ 勉強しているの？じゃあ、_____ 後で話そう。
"Still studying eh? Well, let's talk again after [you are done]."

上司：杉本クン、プロジェクトができたのか。杉本：あの..._____です。
"Boss: Have you finished the project Sugimoto?? Sugimoto: well... not yet..."

奥さん：_____ 残業するか？旦那：仕事が_____終わっていないからだ。
"Wife: Overtime again?? Husband: [It] is because [my] work isn't finished/over yet."

山川さん：是非_____会いましょうよ。友達：はい。では、_____その時に...
Yamakawa: Let's definitely meet up again! Friend: Yes, well then until that time...

ため

Write in the blank whether the ため used in the sentence means "because" or "for the sake of."

彼女が頑張って勉強したため、いい成績を取れた。　　　　　　_____
She　　perservered　studied　　good grades earned

ええ、すごい！これは私のためですか。　　　　　　_____
Wow　awesome　this　　me　　is

日本語を習うためにこの教科書を買った。　　　　　　_____
Japanese　earn　　this　textbook　bought

彼が遅かったため電車を間に合わなかった。　　　　　　_____
He　was slow　　train　　did not make

も vs. もう

Translate the following sentences taking into account the difference between も and もう.

彼(かれ)は彼女(かのじょ)とも別(わか)れた？？ (別れる = to break/split up)

_____

彼(かれ)は彼女(かのじょ)ともう別(わか)れた？

_____

試験(しけん)も失敗(しっぱい)した。 (失敗 = to fail)

_____

試験(しけん)もう失敗(しっぱい)した。

_____

More conditionals 〜たら、ければ

	たら		ければ
いい		いい	
悪<ruby>悪<rt>わる</rt></ruby>い		悪い	
負ける		悪くない	
<ruby>知<rt>し</rt></ruby>る		知らない	
<ruby>死<rt>し</rt></ruby>ぬ		<ruby>遅<rt>おそ</rt></ruby>い	
<ruby>待<rt>ま</rt></ruby>つ		<ruby>速<rt>はや</rt></ruby>くない	
<ruby>会<rt>あ</rt></ruby>う		会わない	
<ruby>信<rt>しん</rt></ruby>じる		<ruby>面白<rt>おもしろ</rt></ruby>い	
だ		でない	
です		<ruby>青<rt>あお</rt></ruby>い	
<ruby>来<rt>く</rt></ruby>る		<ruby>黒<rt>くろ</rt></ruby>い	
<ruby>行<rt>い</rt></ruby>く		行かない	
<ruby>若<rt>わか</rt></ruby>い		若い	

しか vs. だけ

Fill in しか or だけ where appropriate to complete the sentence.

A: どのぐらい残っている？ "About how much is left?"

B: これ＿＿＿＿＿＿です。 "[There] is only this."

A: <ruby>本当<rt>ほんとう</rt></ruby>にこれ＿＿＿＿＿＿<ruby>残<rt>のこ</rt></ruby>っていないか。 "[Is] there truly only this left?"

<ruby>死<rt>し</rt></ruby>ぬまであなた＿＿＿＿＿＿を<ruby>愛<rt>あい</rt></ruby>する！ "[I] will love only you until I die!"

しまった！900<ruby>円<rt>えん</rt></ruby>＿＿＿＿＿＿<ruby>持<rt>も</rt></ruby>っていない。 "Damn! I have only 900 yen."

Making Recommendations

Read the translation and then complete the Japanese sentence to make it a recommendation.

びょうき
病気だから_____。 "Because [you] are sick you should sleep."

しけん　　べんきょう　　　　　はや
試験の勉強があるから早く_____。
"Because [you] have to study [for a] test, [you] should wake up early."

なが　　つ　あ
長く付き合っていないから_____。
"Because [you two] have not been going out for long, [you two] should not get married."

あたま　　いた　　　　くすり
頭が痛ければ薬を_____。
"If [your] head hurts, [you] should drink medicine."

Making Comparisons

Translate the following sentences.

ほう　ぶっか　たか　　おも
オーストラリアの方が物価が高いと思う。
Australia　　　　　　　　prices　high　[I] feel

_____

しゅう　　　　　　　しゅう　ほう　あつ
カリフォルニア州よりアリゾナ州の方が暑いです。
California　　　state　　Arizona　state　　　　　hot　is

_____

体	タイ　からだ　body											
手	シュ　て　hand(s)											
足	ソク　あし　leg(s) & feet　たりる to be sufficient											
耳	ジ　みみ　ear(s)											
心	シン、ジン　こころ　heart, mind, spirit											
医	イ　medical											
薬	ヤク　くすり　medicine											
気	キ、ケ　spirit, air, feeling											
休	キュウ　やすむ　vacation, to take time off, to rest											
血	ケツ　ち　blood											
口	コウ　くち　mouth											
死	シ　death　しぬ　to die											
首	シュウ　くび　neck, neck & head											

女	ジョ　おんな　woman, female										
男	ダン　おとこ　man, male										
内	ナイ　inner, inside　うち　this side, me, mine, my group										
目	モク　め　eye(s)										
用	ヨウ　usage　もちいる　to use, employ										
力	リョク、リキ　ちから　power, strength										
太	タイ　ふとる　to swell, grow fat										
母	ボ　はは、かあ　mother										
父	ジ　ちち、とう　father										
引	イン　ひく　pull										
化	カ、ケ　-ize　ばける　transform into　ばかす　bewitch, transform something										
交	コウ　まぜる　mix, stir, blend　まざる　be mixed　まじる　cross, join										

CHAPTER 13 TRAVEL
第13課

Translate the following sentences into Japanese using either ことにする or ことになる.

I have decided to order udon.

_____。

Because I will go to Japan next year, I have decided to study Japanese.

_____。

It has been decided that I will work on Tuesdays and Thursdays.

_____。

Because he has not taken time off in 3 weeks, it has been decided that he will take today off.

_____。

Because I don't like pork, I have decided that I will eat the shrimp potstickers.

_____。

Translate the following sentences into Japanese using より.

I like music more than movies.

_____。

I like music more than movies, but I will watch this movie.

_____。

This TV is even bigger than [our] last one!

_____。

He is even more famous than the president!

_____。

Fill in the blanks with either そして, それで, それに or それとも to complete dialog.

A: 彼がとてもハンサムだよね。＿＿＿＿＿優しくて子供が好きだと言った。どうすれば

いい？彼に告白した方がいいと思う？＿＿＿＿＿待った方がいいと思う？

B: ま、彼はとても人気があるよね。＿＿＿＿＿彼女がもういるよね。＿＿＿＿＿や

めた方がいいと思うのよ。

Fill in the following chart using your knowledge of the と conditional conjugation.

	と Conjugation	Meaning
いい		
悪い		
負ける		
知る		
死ぬ		
待つ		
会う		
信じる		
だ		
です		
来る		
行く		
若い		

Tack だろう or でしょう onto the end of the following sentences where appropriate given the situation.

(To a friend) 彼女がもう飽きたの＿＿＿＿＿＿。
She may have already gotten sick of [it].

(To a coworker) 課長が私にこのプロジェクトを頼んだの＿＿＿＿＿＿。
The Section Chief asked me to do this project...

(To a supervisor) 佐藤さんは最近毎日働いているから明日は休みを取る＿＿＿＿＿＿。
Mr. Satou has recently been working everyday so perhaps he will take tomorrow off.

Translate the following sentences into Japanese using あげる, もらう, くれる or いただく.

I gave a birthday card to my friend.

＿＿＿＿＿＿＿＿＿＿＿＿＿＿＿＿＿＿＿＿。

Won't you let me have this old book?

＿＿＿＿＿＿＿＿＿＿＿＿＿＿＿＿＿＿＿＿。

I will give you the old book.

＿＿＿＿＿＿＿＿＿＿＿＿＿＿＿＿＿＿＿＿。

I recently received instructions from my boss.

＿＿＿＿＿＿＿＿＿＿＿＿＿＿＿＿＿＿＿＿。

She received a love letter from a boy at school.

＿＿＿＿＿＿＿＿＿＿＿＿＿＿＿＿＿＿＿＿。

Translate the following sentences into Japanese by putting the relevant verb into て form and then tacking on あげる, もらう, くれる or いただく.

I grant this favor for you.

_____。

I will have my underling write the report (for me).

_____。

Will you teach me Japanese?

_____。

She received the benefit of the Division Chief writing a letter of recommendation for her.

_____。

Add the appropriate compound featuring 毎 "every" to complete the sentence.

_____トーストを食べてオレンジジュースを飲んで出かける。
Every morning [I] eat toast, drink orange juice and leave the house.

友達と_____の金曜日にうちで集まって映画を見る。
Every week [I] gather with friend(s) at my place and watch a movie.

お医者さんに行けば_____同じ薬を処方する。
If/when [I] go to the doctor, [the doctor] prescribes the same medicine every time.

Pick clauses which logically go together from the box and link them together into a sentence with the たり pattern. Feel free to modify the verbs as necessary. Next, write the meaning of the sentence you have created in English above the Japanese sentence.

_____。

_____。

_____。

_____。

家に帰る

出かける準備をする

彼女をデートに誘う

テレビを見る

疲れる

友達と会う

コーヒーを買う余裕はない

早起きをする

素敵な一晩を過ごす

最悪だ

ロマンチックな散歩をする

駅で待ち合わせする

映画館で映画を見る

楽しめる

電車が遅れる

旅	リョ　たび　travel, journey
雨	ウ　あめ　rain
夏	カ　なつ　summer
秋	シュウ　あき　fall
冬	トウ　ふゆ　winter
春	シュン　はる　spring
国	コク　くに　country, nation
山	サン　やま　mountain
川	セン　かわ　river
友	ユウ　とも　friend, acquaintance
泳	エイ　およぐ　to swim
空	クウ　empty, sky　そら　sky　あく　to be empty　から　empty
遊	ユウ　recreation　あそぶ　to play, have fun

館 前 後 事 楽 名 泊 留 言 音 写 真	カン　building, facility									
	ゼン　まえ　before, previous, in front of, front									
	ゴ　あと　later, after　うしろ　back, behind									
	ジ　こと　thing (intangible)									
	ラク　relaxing たのしい fun, enjoyable たのしむ to enjoy oneself									
	メイ、ミョウ　な　name									
	ハク・パク　とめる　to give someone shelter　とまる　to stay over									
	リュウ　detain, stay とどめる to stop, stay, limit とどまる to remain, be limited									
	ゲン、ゴン　speech いう to say　こと　word, speech									
	オン　おと　sound									
	シャ　うつす　to transcribe, duplicate, reproduce うつる to be reproduced									
	シン　まこと　true, honest, original									

CHAPTER 14 MAKING PLANS WITH PEOPLE

Pick clauses which logically go together from the box and link them together into a sentence with the し pattern. Feel free to modify the verbs as necessary. Next, write the meaning of the sentence you have created in English above the Japanese sentence.

_____。

_____。

_____。

_____。

いえ　かえ
家に帰る
で　　　　じゅんび
出かける準備をする
かのじょ　　　　　　さそ
彼女をデートに誘う
　　　　　み
テレビを見る
つか
疲れる

ともだち　あ
友達と会う
　　　　　　か　　よゆう
コーヒーを買う余裕はない
はやお
早起きをする
すてき　ひとばん　す
素敵な一晩を過ごす
さいあく
最悪だ

　　　　　　　　さんぽ
ロマンチックな散歩をする
えき　ま　あ
駅で待ち合わせする
えいがかん　えいが　み
映画館で映画を見る
たの
楽しめる
でんしゃ　おく
電車が遅れる

Write in the left-hand boxes whatever combinations of the verbs you think "merge" and then write in the right-hand boxes the combinations you think do not.

		買って帰る Buy+return home
		持って行く Hold/possess + go
		歩いて帰る Walk + return home
		解けていく Melt + go
		食べてみる Eat + see (try)
		返してもらう Return something + for one's benefit
		一晩眠って治った Sleep one night + healed
		腐ったものを食べて吐いた Eat rotten food + vomit

Translate the following sentences into Japanese making use of the つもり grammar form.

I intend to return home and go to bed early.

_____。

Because I will go to Japan next year, I intend to study Japanese.

_____。

Even though I missed my plane, I intend to travel to Spain.

_____。

Translate the following sentences from Japanese into English paying attention to the usage of both あまり and the noun+でいい form.

デートは土曜日の昼でいいですか。

_____。

ごめん、土曜日はちょっと忙しいけど日曜日はあまり忙しくありませんね。

_____。

酒をあまり飲まないから場所はカフェでいいですか。

_____。

Translate the following sentences into Japanese making use of the "anticipation" form.

I am looking forward to spring break!

_____。

Because Mr. Kusanagi has not taken a day off in 3 weeks, he is looking forward to this weekend.

_____。

Were you looking forward to this date?

_____。

Fill in the blanks with either まま, まーまー, or ママ in order to logically complete the dialog.

Mom: この部屋は＿＿＿＿＿暑くないか。窓を開けようか。

Son: いいのよ。閉じた＿＿＿＿＿にして。

Mom: ＿＿＿＿＿は心配しているよ。具合はどう？

Son: 具合は＿＿＿＿＿だけど大丈夫だ。

Mom: 本当にこの＿＿＿＿＿でいいの。

Son: ＿＿＿＿＿、ただの風邪だ。暑い＿＿＿＿＿でいいのよ。

Mom: じゃあ、＿＿＿＿＿は晩御飯を作るから食べたかったら言ってね。

Rewrite the sentences replacing こと with の where appropriate and then translate the sentences into English.

この携帯はGPSが付いていることはとても便利だ。

_____。

_____。

彼女がいつも遅いことが嫌いだ。

_____。

_____。

Verb	Meaning	Verb + こと	Meaning
知る	To know		
歩く	To walk		
帰る	To return home		
待つ	To wait		
見る	To see, watch		
生きる	To live		
死ぬ	To die		
買う	To buy		
売る	To sell		
登る	To climb		

Translate the following sentences into English while taking careful note of the use of verb+こと.

渡辺さんの目的は全てを知ることだ。

_____。

言葉が分からないままで外国に行くことは大変ですよね。

_____。

外国語を学ぶことは偉いと思いますね。

_____。

Paying close attention to the usage of か to connect words or phrases, translate the following sentences into English:

もうだめだ！どうすればいいか分からないのよ。

_____。

彼女は私のことが好きかは知りたい。

_____。

レポートがもうできているか、まだできていないかを彼に聞く。

_____。

Paying close attention to the usage of ていく and てくる, translate the following sentences into English:

買いたい人が多いから値段は上がっていく。

_____。

毎日日本語を勉強したから日本語が少し分かってきた。

_____。

子供のころにクラシックが嫌いだったが、好きになっていくだろう。

_____。

比	ヒ comparative/contrasting くらべる to compare									
品	ヒン しな good(s), item(s)									
買	バイ かう to buy									
売	バイ うる to sell									
店	テン みせ store, shop									
色	ショク color いろ color, sex									
借	シャク debt かりる to borrow									
貸	タイ かす to lend									
返	ヘン かえる to return かえす to return something									
付	フ つく be attached つける to attach									
見	ケン みる to see/look/watch みえる to be able to see みせる to show									
安	アン calm, safe, peace やすい cheap									
長	チョウ boss, main ながい long									

員	イン member										
価	カ value										
客	キャク、カク guest, client, customer										
銀	ギン silver										
商	ショウ trade, commerce										
市	シ City いち market										
場	ジョウ ば place										
所	ショ place ところ point										
持	ジ もつ to have, hold, possess, own										
着	チャク wear, counter for clothing つく to arrive きる to wear										
洋	ヨウ foreign, American/European										
服	フク clothing										

Pick the appropriate verb to end the sentence and then conjugate it into the て form and add おく.

ひこうき　ま　あ
飛行機を間に合うためにアラームを_____。
In order to make the flight, [I] ___ the alarm.

せんせい　おし
先生が教えてくれたことを_____。
[I] will ___ the stuff that my professor taught me.

しけん　ごうかく
試験を合格したいから_____。
Because [I] want to pass the test...

かんが　　　ひま
もう考える暇がないから_____。
Because [I] have no more free time to think...

かんたん　　　　　　　ぶか
簡単なことだから部下に_____。
Because it is a simple matter, [I] will ___ it to my subordinate.

ぜったい　ま　あ　　　　　てがみ　はや
絶対に間に合うために手紙を早めに_____。
In order for the letter to absolutely make it on time, [I] will ___ [it] early.

おぼ 覚える	memorize
べんきょう 勉強する	study
まか 任せる	entrust to
おく 送る	send
せってい 設定する	set
き 決める	decide

Pick the appropriate verb to complete the sentence and then conjugate it into the imperative form.

<ruby>試<rt>し</rt>験<rt>けん</rt></ruby>を<ruby>合<rt>ごう</rt>格<rt>かく</rt></ruby>しなかったからもっと＿＿＿＿＿＿＿＿＿＿＿＿＿＿＿＿＿＿。
Because [I] didn't pass the test [I] need to __ more.

<ruby>用<rt>よう</rt>事<rt>じ</rt></ruby>があるから<ruby>早<rt>はや</rt></ruby>めに＿＿＿＿＿＿＿＿＿＿＿＿＿＿＿＿。
Because [I] have stuff to do, [I] must __.

<ruby>会<rt>かい</rt>議<rt>ぎ</rt></ruby>に＿＿＿＿＿＿＿＿＿＿＿＿＿＿＿＿けど<ruby>行<rt>い</rt></ruby>きたくない。
[I] must __ to the meeting, but [I] don't want to go.

<ruby>全<rt>ぜん</rt>然<rt>ぜん</rt>治<rt>なお</rt></ruby>らないから<ruby>医<rt>い</rt>者<rt>しゃ</rt></ruby>さんと＿＿＿＿＿＿＿＿＿＿＿＿＿。
Because [it] has not healed at all, [I] must __ with the doctor.

アメリカではチップを＿＿＿＿＿＿＿＿＿＿＿＿＿＿。
In America, one must __ tip.

この<ruby>薬<rt>くすり</rt></ruby>を<ruby>一<rt>いち</rt>日<rt>にち</rt></ruby>に<ruby>三<rt>さん</rt>回<rt>かい</rt></ruby>＿＿＿＿＿＿＿＿＿＿＿＿＿＿。
[You] must __ this medicine 3 times in a (per) day.

<ruby>払<rt>はら</rt></ruby>う	pay
<ruby>勉<rt>べん</rt>強<rt>きょう</rt></ruby>する	study
<ruby>飲<rt>の</rt></ruby>む	drink
<ruby>相<rt>そう</rt>談<rt>だん</rt></ruby>する	consult
<ruby>帰<rt>かえ</rt></ruby>る	return home
<ruby>行<rt>い</rt></ruby>く	go

Use ながら to connect two clauses from the list to make a coherent sentence.

＿＿＿＿＿＿＿＿＿＿＿＿＿＿＿＿＿＿＿＿＿＿＿＿＿＿＿＿＿＿。

＿＿＿＿＿＿＿＿＿＿＿＿＿＿＿＿＿＿＿＿＿＿＿＿＿＿＿＿＿＿。

＿＿＿＿＿＿＿＿＿＿＿＿＿＿＿＿＿＿＿＿＿＿＿＿＿＿＿＿＿＿。

<ruby>天<rt>てん</rt>気<rt>き</rt>予<rt>よ</rt>報<rt>ほう</rt></ruby>を<ruby>聞<rt>き</rt></ruby>く
"listen to the weather report"
デザートを<ruby>食<rt>た</rt></ruby>べる "eat dessert"
<ruby>海<rt>かい</rt>外<rt>がい</rt>旅<rt>りょ</rt>行<rt>こう</rt></ruby>の<ruby>準<rt>じゅん</rt>備<rt>び</rt></ruby>をする
"prepare for traveling abroad"

<ruby>宿<rt>しゅく</rt>題<rt>だい</rt></ruby>について<ruby>友<rt>とも</rt>達<rt>だち</rt></ruby>の<ruby>話<rt>はな</rt></ruby>す
"chat about homework with a friend"
<ruby>勉<rt>べん</rt>強<rt>きょう</rt></ruby>する "study"
テレビを<ruby>見<rt>み</rt></ruby>る "watch TV"

Read the following sentences and then write 'C' in the box if you think the しまう adds the nuance of "completion" or write 'M' if you think it adds the nuance of "mistake."

<ruby>誰<rt>だれ</rt></ruby>が <ruby>牛<rt>ぎゅうにゅう</rt></ruby> <ruby>乳<rt></rt></ruby>を <ruby>全部<rt>ぜんぶの</rt></ruby>飲んでしまったの？ _____
Who drank all of the milk?

<ruby>明日<rt>あした</rt></ruby>の <ruby>朝<rt>あさ</rt></ruby>にお <ruby>客<rt>きゃく</rt></ruby> さんとの打ち <ruby>合<rt>う</rt></ruby>わ <ruby>せ<rt>あ</rt></ruby>があることを <ruby>忘<rt>わす</rt></ruby>れてしまった。 _____
[I] forgot about the meeting with the customer tomorrow morning.

<ruby>上 司<rt>じょうし</rt></ruby>の <ruby>前<rt>まえ</rt></ruby>で <ruby>本 当<rt>ほんとう</rt></ruby>の <ruby>意見<rt>いけん</rt></ruby>を <ruby>言<rt>い</rt></ruby>ってしまいました。 _____
[I] said my true opinion in front of my boss.

<ruby>道<rt>みち</rt></ruby>に <ruby>迷<rt>まよ</rt></ruby>って <ruby>郊 外<rt>こうがい</rt></ruby>まで <ruby>行<rt>い</rt></ruby>ってしまった。 _____
[I] was lost and went as far as the suburbs.

<ruby>間違<rt>まちが</rt></ruby>えて <ruby>妹<rt>いもうと</rt></ruby> のクリスマス・プレゼントを <ruby>開<rt>あ</rt></ruby>けてしまった。 _____
[I] mistakenly opened my little sister's Christmas present.

<ruby>常 用 漢 字<rt>じょうようかんじ</rt></ruby>を <ruby>全部覚<rt>ぜんぶおぼ</rt></ruby>えて、 <ruby>旧 漢 字<rt>きゅうかんじ</rt></ruby>まで <ruby>覚<rt>おぼ</rt></ruby>えてしまった。 _____
[I] memorized the standard kanji and went as far as to memorize the ancient kanji.

Translate the following sentences into English keeping in mind the usage of こと.

ブライアンの <ruby>誕 生 日<rt>たんじょうび</rt></ruby> パーティーのことだ。

_____。

11時からの <ruby>会議<rt>かいぎ</rt></ruby>のことです。

_____。

Fill in the chart below, conjugating each verb into the causative, passive and causative-passive forms.

Verb	Meaning	Causative	Passive	Causative-passive
いく	go			
かえる	return home			
はなす	converse			
わかる	understand			
おもう	think/feel			
たべる	eat			
かつ	win			
かく	write			
のむ	drink			
きえる	disappear			
まける	lose			
しぬ	die			
いきる	live			
あそぶ	have fun			
およぐ	swim			
くる	come			
する	do			
あう	meet			
いう	say			
いる	be			
うまれる	be born			
おく	place			
かりる	borrow			
きる	cut			
ふる	shake			
はねる	Jump			

Fill in the chart, conjugating the verbs first into て form commands then into authoritative commands.

Verb	Meaning	Verb in て form	て+ください	Authoritative command
いく	go			
かえる	return home			
はなす	converse			
わかる	understand			
おもう	think/feel			
たべる	eat			
かつ	win			
かく	write			
のむ	drink			
きえる	disappear			
まける	lose			
しぬ	die			
いきる	live			
あそぶ	have fun			
およぐ	swim			
くる	come			
する	do			
あう	meet			
いう	say			
いる	be			
うまれる	be born			
おく	place			
かりる	borrow			
きる	cut			
ふる	shake			
はねる	Jump			

Pick the appropriate sound word from the list to complete each sentence.

ときどき	occasionally, from time to time	べつべつ	Separately
たまたま	unexpectedly, by chance	ばたばた	Flapping, commotion (being busy)
ドキドキ	heart pounding	バラバラ	scattered, in pieces, disparate
きらきら	bright, shining, sparkly	びしょびしょ	wet, soaked through
ぺらぺら	fluency in a language	こそこそ	Sneakily, stealthily, whisper
ぐずぐず	slow, lazily	ザーザー	heavy rainfall
わくわく	thrill, excitement	ぼろぼろ	Worn, crumbling, dilapidated

飲み物を溢してズボンが_____になった。
[I] spilled [my] drink and my pants became __.

道に迷って諦めるところに_____行き先に着いた。
[I] was lost and at the point of giving up, [I] __ arrived at [my] destination.

今日はすることが一杯あるから_____しないで！
Today [we] have lots to do so don't __.

彼は仕事をしながら一人で子供を育てているからいつも_____しているよね。
Because he is working while raising a child by himself, he is always __.

カフェでコーヒーを飲みながら雨が_____降ることを聞いた。
While drinking coffee at the café, [I] heard the rain fall __.

ジェフくんは日本語が_____ですよ。
Jeff is __ in Japanese.

Fill in the chart first giving the stem, then the verb plus かた and then the new meaning.

Verb	Meaning	Verb stem	Verb stem +かた	Meaning
いく	go			
かえる	return home			
はなす	converse			
わかる	understand			
おもう	think/feel			
たべる	eat			
かつ	win			
かく	write			
のむ	drink			
きえる	disappear			
まける	lose			
しぬ	die			
いきる	live			
あそぶ	have fun			
およぐ	swim			
くる	come			
する	do			
あう	meet			
いう	say			
いる	be			
うまれる	be born			
おく	place			
かりる	borrow			
きる	cut			
ふる	shake			
はねる	Jump			

Fill in the blank in each sentence with either 間 or 内 as appropriate.

先生が見ていない＿＿＿＿ 隣 に座っている学生とこそこそ話した。
While the teacher wasn't looking, [I] conversed in whisper with the student sitting next to me.

普通電車に乗っている＿＿＿＿にたばこを吸ってはいけません。
While riding a regular train, one may not smoke.

数学のレクチャーの＿＿＿＿ずっとノートを取りました。
[I] took notes all the while listening to the lecture on mathematics.

彼女と真剣なことについて話している＿＿＿＿ 急 に笑ってしまった。
While talking about something serious with her, [I] suddenly laughed.

仕	シ to attend, to serve													
動	ドウ　うごく　to move													
働	ドウ　はたらく　to work													
工	コウ　craft, construction													
材	ザイ　materials													
作	サク　つくる　to make													
使	シ　つかう　to use													
会	シャ　company, office, association													
書	ショ　かく to write													
方	ホウ　direction　かた　way of doing, a person (honorific)													
法	ホウ　law, order, way of doing													
聞	ブン、モン　news　きく　to ask, to listen　きこえる　to be able to hear													
問	モン　とう　to ask													

業	ギョウ business, vocation, performance											
不	フ、ブ not, negative, poor, badly											
通	ツウ transport, pass　とおる to pass through　とおす make go through　かよう to commute											
運	ウン fate, karma　はこぶ to carry, to transport											
建	ケン construction, skeleton　たてる to construct　たつ to be constructed											
送	ソウ おくる to send, transmit, mail											
研	ケン study　とぐ to polish, sharpen											
究	キュウ research, study											
勤	キン つとめる to be employed											
終	シュウ おえる to finish something　おわる to end, for something to finish											
世	セ、セイ よ generation, world, society											
界	カイ world											

Pick a phrase to tack onto the end of the provided clause to create a (logical) sentence while using the proper conjunction ので or のに with particle な where necessary.

ちょうし わる
調子が悪くなっています condition is worsening

しゅくだい わす
宿題を忘れてしまった forgot homework

まいにちじゅぎょう こ
ちゃんと毎日授業に来ない does not come everyday

ひろ かん
あまり広く感じない does not feel spacious

ともだち
友達がたくさんいる has many friends

つく
なんでも作れる can make anything

ま
負けたことはない has never lost

かね
そんなに金がない do not have that kind of money

かれ
彼はハンサム＿＿＿＿＿＿＿＿＿＿＿＿。
He [is] handsome

せいせき
あさみちゃんの成績はいい＿＿＿＿＿＿＿＿＿＿＿＿。
Asami's grades [are] good

くるま せかいじゅう いちばんはや
この車は世界中で一番早い＿＿＿＿＿＿＿＿＿＿＿＿。
This car [is] the fastest in the world

せんせい かんじゃ お
先生、患者が起きました＿＿＿＿＿＿＿＿＿＿＿＿。
Doctor, the patient [has] woken

まつもと りょうり ひと
松本さんは料理がうまい人＿＿＿＿＿＿＿＿＿＿＿＿。
Mrs. Matsumoto is a person who is great at cooking

あたら くるま か
新しい車を買いたい＿＿＿＿＿＿＿＿＿＿＿＿。
[I] want to buy a new car

にかいだ いえ
二階建ての家＿＿＿＿＿＿＿＿＿＿＿＿。
[It is] a 2 story house

がっこう い
学校まで行った＿＿＿＿＿＿＿＿＿＿＿＿。
[I] went as far as school

Fill in the blanks with what you feel would logically complete the sentence.

このドレスと合う＿＿（コート）＿＿を探している。　"[I am] looking for a <u>coat</u> that goes with this dress."

このケーキと合う＿＿＿＿＿＿＿＿＿＿を作っている。
Go with this cake　　　　　　　　making

この髪のカットは＿＿＿＿＿＿＿＿と合わないよね。
This haircut　　　　　　　　doesn't go well with eh?

素敵なカップルなので＿＿＿＿＿＿＿が合っているよね。
Amazing couple so　　　　　　　goes well together eh?

赤色は＿＿＿＿＿＿＿＿と合う。
The color red　　　　　go with

渡辺さんは頑固だから＿＿＿＿＿＿＿＿と合うかな。
Because Mrs. Watanabe is stubborn　　[I] wonder if [she] goes with

Translate the following simple English sentences into Japanese using the かどうか construction.

_____
I do not know if I will go to the party or not.

_____
I do not know if the train will come at 4:30 or not.

_____
I will check whether the movie will be over by 7pm or not.

_____
Because she has never eaten sushi, she does not know if she likes it or not.

_____
I have not decided whether I will quit my job or not.

Translate the following simple English sentences into Japanese using the ように construction.

_____

I will save money in order to be able to go on vacation.

_____

She studied for three days in order to pass the test.

_____

Mr. Yamaguchi will go to Germany in order to study German.

_____

I will study in order to learn Japanese.

_____

He said that he will not cooperate to make the project a success.

Conjugate the verb at the end of each sentence into either ている、てある、ておる as appropriate, crossing out any unnecessary hiragana and adjusting the level of speech where necessary.

<ruby>彼<rt>かの</rt></ruby><ruby>女<rt>じょ</rt></ruby>の<ruby>絵<rt>え</rt></ruby>が<ruby>壁<rt>かべ</rt></ruby>に<ruby>掛<rt>か</rt></ruby>かる_____。 "Her painting is hanging on the wall."

お<ruby>腹<rt>なか</rt></ruby>が<ruby>空<rt>す</rt></ruby>いたからあきとくんが<ruby>食<rt>た</rt></ruby>べる_____。 "Because he is hungry, Akito is eating."

<ruby>床<rt>とこ</rt></ruby>の<ruby>間<rt>ま</rt></ruby>にいけばなが<ruby>飾<rt>かざ</rt></ruby>る_____。 "A flower arrangement is displayed in the alcove."

(to one's boss) <ruby>報告<rt>ほうこく</rt></ruby>を<ruby>書<rt>か</rt></ruby>く_____。 "[I am] writing [the] report."

(to one's teacher) <ruby>教<rt>おし</rt></ruby>えてくれたことを<ruby>覚<rt>おぼ</rt></ruby>える_____。
"[I] remember what you taught me."

<ruby>会議<rt>かいぎ</rt></ruby>に<ruby>遅<rt>おく</rt></ruby>れる_____。 "[I am] late to the meeting."

<ruby>電気<rt>でんき</rt></ruby>がつける_____。 "The light is on."

Using はず finish the Japanese sentences according to the English translations.

大阪に行く電車はもうすぐ来る＿＿＿＿＿＿＿＿＿＿。
The train to Osaka will likely come pretty soon now.

彼女がこんなところにいる＿＿＿＿＿＿＿＿＿＿。
It is very unlikely that she will be in this kind of place.

先生が間違えた＿＿＿＿＿＿＿＿＿＿。
It is unlikely the professor made a mistake.

松島さんは危険を分かっている＿＿＿＿＿＿＿＿＿＿。
Mr. Matsushima likely understands the danger.

犯罪者は警察に捕まる＿＿＿＿＿＿＿＿＿＿。
Criminals will likely be caught by the cops.

Complete the following sentences by adding the appropriate word + でも.

松本さんは料理がうまいから＿＿＿＿＿＿作れる。
Because Mrs. Matsumoto is skilled at cooking, she can make anything.

＿＿＿＿＿＿＿に入るため入場料を払わなければならない。
An entrance fee must be paid to get into even there.

好きなものは＿＿＿＿＿＿＿あげるよ。
[I] will give [you] whichever you want.

子供の卒業式は＿＿＿＿＿＿＿行けるイベントではありません。
[Your] child's graduation is not an event you can go to anytime.

彼は＿＿＿＿＿＿＿と付き合わないからちょっとうらやましい。
He will not go out with just anyone so [I am] a little jealous.

111

Complete the following sentences by adding the appropriate word + か or も.

松本さんは料理がうまいから＿＿＿＿＿＿＿を作ってくれる。
Because Mrs. Matsumoto is skilled at cooking, she will make something for you.

石村さんは＿＿＿＿＿＿＿ 忙しい。
Mr. Ishimura is always busy.

結婚記念日だから＿＿＿＿＿＿＿に行こうよ。
Because [it's our] wedding anniversary, let's go somewhere.

何回電話したのに＿＿＿＿＿＿＿電話に出なかった。
Even though [I] called several times, no one answered the phone.

途中でエンジンが＿＿＿＿＿＿＿壊れたので飛行機を間に合わなかった。
Part way there, the engine died for some reason so I did not make the flight.

Fill in the blank with the appropriate variation of 言う and any necessary particles.

「sneak」は日本語でどう＿＿＿＿＿＿＿？ How [do I] say "sneak" in Japanese?

彼はすしが好きだ＿＿＿＿＿＿＿のにあまり食べない。
Even though he says [he] likes sushi, [he] doesn't eat [sushi] much.

日本語が簡単だと誰も＿＿＿＿＿＿＿。 No one says that Japanese is easy.

アニキ＿＿＿＿＿＿＿映画を探している。 [I] am looking for a movie called "Aniki."

ここがエリア５１＿＿＿＿＿＿＿秘密の基地ですか。 [So] this is the secret base called Area 51?

Complete the following sentences by adding the appropriate variation of かもしれない.

このぐらいのガスで行ける＿＿＿＿＿＿＿＿＿＿＿。

(to one's henchman) 秘密兵器で敵を倒せる＿＿＿＿＿＿＿＿＿＿＿。

(to one's boss) 来年までに売り上げを１２％上げることができる＿＿＿＿＿＿＿＿＿＿＿。

藤本さんは先に帰った＿＿＿＿＿＿＿＿＿＿＿。

招	ショウ　まねく　to invite
広	コウ　ひろい　wide, open　ひろめる　to spread　ひろまる　be spread　ひろげる　to widen　ひろがる　be widened
自	ジ　oneself
他	タ　ほか　other, outside, separate
初	ショ　はじめて　first time
始	シ　はじめる　to begin something　はじまる　for something to begin
新	シン　あたらしい　new
古	コ　ふるい　old, used, ancient
者	シャ　もの　person, a peoples
主	シュ　main　ぬし　master　おもな　main
意	イ　opinion
味	ミ　あじ　flavor
実	ジツ　real, actual　み　fruit of one's labor, (actual) fruit

住	ジュウ　すむ　to reside											
族	ゾク　family, tribe, group											
親	シン　おや　parent(s)											
帰	キ　かえる　to return home											
茶	チャ　さ　tea											
兄	キョウ　あに　my older brother　にい　older brother											
姉	シ　あね　my older sister　ねえ　older sister											
弟	ダイ　おとうと　younger brother											
妹	マイ　いもうと　younger sister											
紹	ショウ　introduce, inherit											
介	カイ　mediate, concern oneself with-											
知	チ　knowledge　しる　to know/hear of something											

Answers

Chapter 2
T, T, F, T, F, T, F, T, T

これはペンだ。 = simply, "This is a pen."
これがペンだ。 = "*This* (as opposed to whatever else) is a pen."
彼女の名前は笑みだ。 = simply "Her name is Emi."
彼女の名前が笑みだ。 = "*Her* name (as opposed to some other girl's name) is Emi."

The subjects of the sentences are: これ, そちらのお方, 部屋を出た人, 日曜日,
毎週の月曜日, 毎週, 毎週

The omitted subjects are:
私は, 私は, 私は, あなたは

Directional Particles

映画館に行く。 "[I will] go to the movie theater."

家に帰る。 "[I will] return to [my] home."

職場へ行くの。 "[Will you] go to [your] workplace?"

昼ご飯にカレーを食べた。 "[I] ate curry for lunch."

友達にプレゼントをあげる。 "[I will] give a present to [my] friend."

彼女にプレゼントをもらった。 "[I] received a present from her."

これは彼女からもらったチョコだ。 "This is chocolate [I] received from her."

Compound Particles には, への and からの

私には数学が楽しいです。 "To me, math is fun."

月曜日には会議がある。 "There is a meeting on Monday."

友達へのプレゼントだ。 "This is a present to/for [my] friend."

友達からの手紙だ。 "This is a letter from [my] friend."

Connecting Verbs with Particle を
を, を, X, X, を, X

Asking Questions with Particles か, かい and の
か, かい, の, か, の, か, か, か

Signifying a relationship between two nouns with の
これは私のリュックです。　(possessive relationship)　"This is my backpack."
不幸の手紙をもらった。　(descriptive relationship)　"[I] received an unlucky (unfortunate) letter."

Ending a sentence with のか or のだ
のか, のだ, のか, のだ, のだ

Particle で
公園でピックニックする。　　　　"[I/we will] picnic *at* the park."
来月に引っ越す。　　　　　　　"[I will] move home next month."
自分でやった。　　　　　　　　"[I] did [it] *by* myself."
今年はタバコをやめる。　　　　　"[I will] quit smoking this year."
家でゆっくり過ごす。　　　　　　"[I/we will] spend time leisurely *at* the house."
車で友達の家に行った。　　　　　"[I] went to [my] friend's house *by* car."

Listing things with Particles と, とか, も and や
中国の映画と日本の映画と韓国の映画が好きだ。
中国の映画とか韓国の映画とかが好きだ。
中国の映画や韓国の映画が好きだ。
中国の映画も日本の映画も韓国の映画も好きだ。

Other uses of Particle と
彼は日本語が難しいと言った。
日本語が難しいと彼が言った。
語学はちょっと難しいと思う。

彼女と[私]の関係は全くない。　(possessive)
Lit. "[The] relationship of her and I does not exist at all." i.e. "We have absolutely nothing to do with each other."
ジャズとクラシックとの違いは色々ある。(possessive)　"[There] are various differences between Jazz and classical music.
私と彼とのデートはとても楽しかった。(possessive) "[The] date with her and myself was very enjoyable."

Chapter 3

昨日はとても楽しい日だった。　宮本さんはいい人だ。

彼女は彼がためたお金を全部使った。　[私は]使う前にフライパンをきれいに洗った。

日本語の授業は週に三回集まる。　彼は大きいな問題がある。

私は明日は日本語の試験がある。

今日は休みだ。　　私は友達に/からプレゼントをもらった。

来週に彼女とデートをする。　　　日本語の授業が好きだ。

昨日は楽しかった。　私は二人の友達にプレゼントをあげる。

私は来年に日本に留学する。　　彼はイカが好きじゃない。

Chapter 4

Plain pos futr	かつ	まける	いく	する
Plain negative	かたない	まけない	いかない	しない
Plain past	かった	まけた	いった	した
Plain past neg	かたなかった	まけなかった	いかなかった	しなかった
Lesser polite	かちます	まけます	いきます	します
Polite negative	かちません	まけません	いきません	しません
Polite past	かちました	まけました	いきました	しました
Polite past neg	かちませんでした	まけませんでした	いきませんでした	しませんでした

Plain pos futr	くる	だ	いる	ある
Plain negative	こない	で/じゃ/では+ない	いない	ない
Plain past	きた	だった	いた	あった
Plain past neg	こなかった	で/じゃ/では+なかった	いなかった	なかった
Lesser polite	きます	です	います	あります
Polite negative	きません	で/じゃ/では+ありません	いません	ありません
Polite past	きました	でした	いました	ありました
Pol past neg	きませんでした	で/じゃ/では+ありませんでした	いませんでした	ありませんでした

Plain pos futr	べんり [だ]	いい	すごい	はで [だ]
Plain negative	べんりじゃない	よくない	すごくない	はでじゃない
Plain past	べんりだった	よかった	すごかった	はでだった
Plain past neg	べんりじゃなかった	よくなかった	すごくなかった	はでじゃなかった
Lesser polite	べんりです	いいです	すごいです	はでです
Polite negative	べんりじゃありません	よくありません	すごくありません	はでじゃありません
Polite past	べんりでした	よかったです	すごかったです	はででした
Pol past neg	べんりじゃありませんでした	よくありませんでした	すごくありませんでした	はでじゃありませんでした

いて、いって、のって、とって、あげて、くれて、もらって、しんじて、かって、まけて、
よんで、やって、ねて、のぼって、まがって、かんがえて、おぼえて、くださって、おもって、そだって、まなんで、しんで、およいで、はなして

はでで、つよくて、よわくて、あたらしくて、ふるくて、きれいで、やさしくて、やすくて、たかくて、
ふくざつで、きびしくて、はやくて、おそくて、へんで、おかしくて、たのしくて、おもしろくて

Chapter 5

Family names:
松本、井上、武田、佐藤、鈴木、中山、島村、山本、小林、富士、内藤、斉藤、川崎、杉本、田中、高橋
Given names:
愛、明美、千代、恵子、由美、恵美、和也、信夫、三郎、茂、隆、剛、義雄、健太、健太郎、陽子

none, none, none, none, さん, さん, さま, さん, くん, ちゃん

Y, N, Y, Y, Y

これの本、それの本、あれの本、どれの本
この本、その本、あの本、どの本
こんな本、そんな本、あんな本、どんな本
ここ、そこ、あそこ、どこ
こっち/こちらの本、そっち/そちらの本、あっち/あちらの本、どっち/どちらの本

こんにちは、おはよう、今晩は、おはようございます、おはようございます、久しぶりですね。
久しぶり〜！

では〜、じゃあね〜！、じゃあね！、(nothing/nod/other gesture)、またね、
また会いましょうよ！

(Depending on rank) 杉本さん、杉本 係 長 (かかりちょう)
中島課長、高橋さん or さちこちゃん or some nickname like さっちゃん (if you are close friends)
誠くん or まっちゃん、夏子ちゃん or なっちゃん

どうも、nothing、どうもありがとうございます or 感 謝 (かんしゃ) しております、ありがとう、ありがとうございます

失礼します、すみません or ごめんなさい、ごめんなさい、
ごめんなさい or 申し訳ありません (introduced in CH11)、ごめんね

Paying attention, affirmative, affirmative, refusal, affirmative, refusal

Chapter 6

こちらは金田さんです。この人(or 方^{かた})は池田さんです。宮元です。よろしくお願いします。
はじめまして、宮元です。こちらは課長の山本さんです。**or** こちらは山本課長です。

127 = 百二十七 （ひゃくにじゅうなな/しち）
43,689 = 四万三千六百八十九 （よんまんさんぜんろっぴゃくはちじゅうきゅう）
2,540,864 = 二百五十四万八百六十四 （にひゃくごじゅうよんまんはっぴゃくろくじゅうよん）

四枚 （よんまい）　三本 （さんぼん）　二台 （にだい）　十回 （じゅっかい）
十四人 （じゅうよんにん）　一軒 （いっけん）　二十七階 （にじゅうなな/しちかい）
二千四百円 （にせんよんひゃくえん）　五個 （ごこ）

一月の四日 （いちがつのよっか）　二千十年の十一月 （にせんじゅうねんのじゅういちがつ）
五月十九日の土曜日 （ごがつじゅうくにちのどようび）

午前五時半 （ごぜんごじはん）　十八時 （じゅうはちじ）or 午後六時 （ごごろくじ）
十一時 （じゅういちじ）

二年間 （にねんかん）　一週間 （いっしゅうかん）　一時間半 （いちじかんはん）
三十五分 （さんじゅうごふん）　三ヶ月間 （さんかげつかん）　四時間 （よんじかん）
一日 （いちにち）　一日中 （いちにちちゅう）　六日間 （むいかかん）

二千十一年十一月二日 （にせんじゅういちねんじゅういちがつふつか）
千九百九十三年二月十二日 （せんきゅうひゃくきゅうじゅうさんねんにがつじゅうににち）
千九百八十一年八月六日 （せんきゅうひゃくはちじゅういちねんはちがつむいか）
千九百一年十二月二十五日 （せんきゅうひゃくいちねんじゅうにがつにじゅうごにち）
二千年一月一日 （にせんいちねんいちがつついたち）
千九百九十九年九月二十日 （せんきゅうひゃくきゅうじゅうきゅうねんくがつはつか）
千九百八十六年三月二十日 （せんきゅうひゃくはちじゅうろくねんさんがつはつか）
千九百九十一年六月十日 （せんきゅうひゃくきゅうじゅういちねんろくがつとおか）
二千五年五月五日 （にせんごねんごがつついつか）

Chapter 7

はなす＝う、はなしている、はなしています　　いく＝irregular、いっている、いっています
あるく＝う、あるいている、あるいています　　およぐ＝う、およいでいる、およいでいます
はしる＝う、はしっている、はしっています　　のむ＝う、のんでいる、のんでいます
たべる＝る、たべている、たべています　　　あげる＝る、あげている、あげています
よむ＝う、よんでしる、よんでいます　　　　おぼえる＝る、おぼえている、おぼえています
そだつ＝う、そだっている、そだっています　　まける＝る、まけている、まけています
かつ＝う、かっている、かっています　　　　あわせる＝る、あわせている、あわせています
しんじる＝る、しんじている、しんじています　ねる＝る、ねている、ねています
なる＝う、なっている、なっています　　　　かんがえる＝る、かんがえている、かんがえています
あう＝う、あっている、あっています　　　　しぬ＝う、しんでいる、しんでいます
よぶ＝う、よんでいる、よんでいます　　　　くる＝irregular、きている、きています

F, B, B, B, F, F

が、けど、けど、けど

来て、聞いてください、読んでください、出して

To family: 弟、妹、お兄さん、お姉さん、お母さん、お父さん、叔父さん、叔母さん、伯父さん、伯母さん、お祖母さん、お祖父さん、妻、夫/旦那
To someone else: 弟、妹、兄、姉、母、父、叔父さん、叔母さん、伯父さん、伯母さん、祖母、祖父、妻、夫/旦那
To that person: ＿さん、＿さん、＿さん、＿さん、お母さん (or さま for the rest)、お父さん、叔父さん、叔母さん、伯父さん、伯母さん、お祖母さん、お祖父さん、奥さん、旦那さん
To another family member: 弟さん、妹さん、お兄さん、お姉さん、お母さん、お父さん、叔父さん、叔母さん、伯父さん、伯母さん、お祖母さん、お祖父さん、奥さん、旦那さん

行って来る、行って来ます、行って来ます、ただいま、ただいま、お帰り、お帰りなさい、お帰り、行っていらっしゃい、nothing, (or if you're a modern guy) 行っていらっしゃい

青（あお）い、上（うえ）、横（よこ）、前（まえ）、色（いろ）、紺（こん）、紺（こん）、緑（みどり）、赤（あか）い、右（みぎ）

Chapter 8

Money, time/# of stops, time/distance, time/effort

Shizuoka Prefecture, Shizuoka City, Suruga Ward, Tsushima Neighborhood, Division 3, Subdivision 2, Bldg #3, room 405
Aichi Prefecture, Nagoya City, Higashi (East) Ward, Yamaguchi Neighborhood, Division 2, Subdivision 4, Bldg #1, room 216

番、番、一番、一番

朝に8時に起きる。　漫画が好きです。　いいえ、すしを食べます。　山口駅で止まりますよ。

どうやって、どうした、どうして、どうして、どうした、どうやって

よくない、いい/よいです、よくないです/よくありません、よかった、よくなかった、よかったです、よくなかったです/よくありませんでした

よくなかったね！　よく

(blank)、と思う、と思う、と思う

Chapter 9

食べに行く。　会いに行く。　しに来た。　調べに来た。

食べてほしい。　片付けてほしい。　見てほしい。　着替えてほしい。　読んでほしい。

それでも、なんでも、だれでも、どうでも

いい、よくないです、よくなかった

喋ってください、考えてください、話して、思わない、言った、言った、思います、考えた

後に、前に、後に、前に

Chapter 10

飲みたい　"I want to drink"　　　飲んでほしい　"I want [someone else] to drink"
知りたい　"I want to know"　　　知ってほしい　"I want [someone else] to know"
運転したい　"I want to drive"　　運転してほしい　"I want [someone else] to drive"
買いたい　"I want to buy"　　　　買ってほしい　"I want [someone else] to buy"
任せたい　"I want to delegate to someone"　任せてほしい　"I want someone to delegate to me"

お腹が空いた or 腹が減った、お腹が空きました、腹が減った、お腹が空いた

はなす＝う、はなし、はなそう、はなしましょう　　いく＝う、いき、いこう、いきましょう
あるく＝う、あるき、あるこう、あるきましょう　　およぐ＝う、およぎ、およごう、およぎましょう
はしる＝う、はしり、はしろう、はしりましょう　　のむ＝う、のみ、のもう、のみましょう
たべる＝る、たべ、たべよう、たべましょう　　あげる＝る、あげ、あげよう、あげましょう
よむ＝う、よみ、よもう、よみましょう　　おぼえる＝る、おぼえ、おぼえよう、おぼえましょう
そだつ＝う、そだち、そだとう、そだちましょう　　まける＝る、まけ、まけよう、まけましょう
かつ＝う、かち、かとう、かちましょう　　ねる＝る、ね、ねよう、ねましょう
なる＝う、なり、なろう、なりましょう　　あわせる＝る、あわせ、あわせよう、あわせましょう
あう＝う、あい、あおう、あいましょう　　しんじる＝る、しんじ、しんじよう、しんじましょう
かんがえる＝る、かんがえ、かんがえよう、かんがえましょう　くる＝irr、き、こよう、きましょう
しぬ＝う、しに、しのう、しにましょう　　よぶ＝う、よび、よぼう、よびましょう
する＝irr、し、しよう、しましょう　　あそぶ＝う、あそび、あそぼう、あそびましょう
いう＝う、いい、いおう、いいましょう　　いる＝irr、い、いよう、いましょう
うまれる＝る、うまれ、うまれよう、うまれましょう　　おく＝う、おき、おこう、おきましょう
かりる＝る、かり、かりよう、かりましょう　　きる＝う、きり、きろう、きましょう
ふる＝う、ふり、ふろう、ふりましょう

はなす＝う、はなし、はなせば　　いく＝う、いき、いけば
あるく＝う、あるき、あるけば　　およぐ＝う、およぎ、およげば
はしる＝う、はしり、はしれば　　のむ＝う、のみ、のめば
たべる＝る、たべ、たべれば　　あげる＝る、あげ、あげれば
よむ＝う、よみ、よめば　　おぼえる＝る、おぼえ、おぼえれば
そだつ＝う、そだち、そだてば　　まける＝る、まけ、まければ
かつ＝う、かち、かてば　　ねる＝る、ね、ねれば
なる＝う、なり、なれば　　あわせる＝る、あわせ、あわせれば
あう＝う、あい、あえば　　しんじる＝る、しんじ、しんじれば
かんがえる＝る、かんがえ、かんがえれば　　くる＝irr、き、くれば
しぬ＝う、しに、しねば　　よぶ＝う、よび、よべば　　する＝irr、し、すれば
あそぶ＝う、あそび、あそべば　　いう＝う、いい、いえば　　いる＝irr、い、いれば
うまれる＝る、うまれ、うまれば　　おく＝う、おき、おけば　　かりる＝る、かり、かりれば
きる＝う、きり、きれば　　ふる＝う、ふり、ふれば

Possible combinations:　最高にする、無駄にする、すしにする、ケーキにする、デザートにする、最後にする、好きにする、ジュースにする

メキシコに行ったことがある？　刺身を食べたことがある？　歌を歌ったことがある？
うわさをしたことがある？

メキシコに行ったことがある/ない。刺身を食べたことがある/ない。歌を歌ったことがある/ない。
うわさをしたことがある/ない。

パン、飲み、遊び、スキーをし、すし、きれい、話し、返し

Chapter 11

先（さき）に行（い）ってもいい[ですか]。　午後六時（ごごろくじ）に帰（かえ）ってもいい[ですか]。
宿題（しゅくだい）を少（すこ）し遅（おそ）くて出（だ）してもいい[ですか]。　質問（しつもん）をしてもいい[ですか]。

今（いま）はトイレに行（い）ってはだめだ。or 今（いま）はトイレに行（い）ってはいけない/いけません。
試験（しけん）を始（はじ）めてもいい[です]。　木曜日（もくようび）に早（はや）めに帰（かえ）ってもいい[です]。
試験（しけん）の期間（きかん）が終（お）わるまで出（で）てはだめだ　or　試験（しけん）の期間（きかん）が終（お）わるまで出（で）てはいけない/いけません。

ダイエットをしようかなと思（おも）っている。　たかしは海（うみ）に行（い）こうかなと思（おも）っていた。
友達（ともだち）と一緒（いっしょ）に勉強（べんきょう）しようかなと思（おも）っている。　実家（じっか）に帰（かえ）ろうかなと思（おも）っている。

もっと勉強（べんきょう）してみる。　納豆（なっとう）を食（た）べてみる。　職場（しょくば）に歩（ある）いて行（い）ってみる。　彼（かれ）と話（はな）してみる。

勉強（べんきょう）しなかったので試験（しけん）を合格（ごうかく）しなかった。彼女（かのじょ）が宿題（しゅくだい）を忘（わす）れたので先生（せんせい）が怒（おこ）った。
今日（きょう）は元気（げんき）なので遊（あそ）びたいんだ。明日（あした）は忙（いそが）しいので何（なに）もできない。

きれいなのに好きじゃない。　彼が遅いのに少し待とう/待ちましょう。
よく読むのにまだ分からない。　彼が有名じゃないのに好きだ。

はなす＝う、はなせる、はなせ　　いく＝う、いける、いけ
あるく＝う、あるける、あるけ　　およぐ＝う、およげる、およげ
はしる＝う、はしれる、はしれ　　のむ＝う、のめる、のめ
たべる＝る、たべれる、たべ　　　あげる＝る、あげれる、あげ
よむ＝う、よめる、よめ　　　　　おぼえる＝る、おぼえれる、おぼえれ
そだつ＝う、そだてる、そだて　　まける＝る、まけれる、まけれ
かつ＝う、かてる、かて　　　　　ねる＝る、ねれる、ねれ
なる＝う、なれる、なれ　　　　　あわせる＝る、あわせれる、あわせれ
あう＝う、あえる、あえ　　　　　しんじる＝る、しんじれる、しんじれ
かんがえる＝る、かんがえれる、かんがえれ　　　くる＝irr、これる、これ
しぬ＝う、しねる、しね　　　　　よぶ＝う、よべる、よべ　　する＝irr、できる、でき
あそぶ＝う、あそべる、あそべ　　いう＝う、いえる、いえ　　いる＝irr、いれる or いられる、いれ
うまれる＝る、うまれれる、うまれれ　　おく＝う、おける、おけ　　かりる＝る、かりれる、かりれ
きる＝う、きれる、きれ　　　　　ふる＝う、ふれる、ふれ

歩くことができますか。　酒を飲めますか。　払えますよ。　食べることができる。
指で読むことができるのよ。　日本語を読めますか。　とても速く走れる。　走ることができない。

漢字はとても覚えにくい[です]。　学校で新しい友達を作りやすい[です]。
友達はチェスはとても上手だから勝ちにくい[です]。　子供を育てにくい[です]。
昔の英語はとても読みにくい[です]。　彼女はとても頭がいいから信じやすい[です]。
急な登り道だから落ちて怪我をしやすい[です]。　新しい仕事に慣れにくい[です]。

忙しくなる、become busy。　駄目にする、make a mess (screw something up badly)
速い、帰る、return home quickly　完全、終わらせる、completely finish something
嫌いになる　完璧、できる　ばらばらに切る　遅く寝る、go to bed late
深く感じる　静かに話す、converse quietly　よくある、to have/occur a lot, frequent happening
永く走る、run for a long time

Chapter 12

だから、からだ、からです、だから

(1st sentence) Could use ようだ，そうだ, or らしい depending on whether the speaker is judging based on say the listener's appearance (bling) or what a mutual friend might have said.

ビジネスはうまく行っているようだ。 The translation says "must be" which sounds more like an observation the speaker is making.

来年から飛行機のチケットが高くなるそうだ。 This isn't the kind of thing one is likely to notice firsthand, so the speaker likely read it in the newspaper etc.

Could use なそうだ or らしい since this is likely something the speaker heard.

この豆腐が腐っているようだ。 This is obviously a direct observation.

Could use なそうだ or らしい since this is likely based off a rumor that the speaker heard.

Could use なそうだ or らしい since this is once again likely based off of rumor or perhaps an article in a newspaper etc.

田中さんはサッカー部を辞めるそうだ。 山田さんの車はまた壊れたようだね！
あのアプリがとても役に立つらしい。 そのデパートにある店は高いらしいですよ。
あの歌手はメキシコ人なようだ。 あのレストランの店内はとてもはでなそうです。

まだ、また、まだまだ、また、まだ、また、また

because, for, for, because

He broke up with *even her!?*   He broke up with her *already!?*
[I] failed even [this] test.   [I've] already failed [this] test.

よかったら、悪かったら、負けたら、知ったら、死んだら、待ったら、会ったら、信じたら、だったら、
でしたら、きたら、行ったら、若かったら
よければ、悪ければ、悪くなければ、知らなければ、遅ければ、速くなければ、会わなければ、面白ければ、
でなければ、青ければ、黒ければ、行かなければ、若ければ

だけ、しか、だけ、しか

病気だから寝た方がいい[です]。 試験の勉強があるから早く起きた方がいい[です]。
長く付き合っていないから結婚しない方がいい[です]。 頭が痛ければ薬を飲んだ方がいい[です]。

I feel/think that prices are higher in Australia.   Arizona is hotter than California.

Chapter 13

うどんを注文することにした。　来年に日本に行くから日本語を勉強することにした。
火曜日と木曜日に働くことになった。　彼は3週間に休みを取っていないから今日は休むことになった。
豚肉が好きじゃないからえび餃子を食べることにした。

音楽が映画より好きだ。　or　映画より音楽の方が好きだ。
音楽が映画より好きだけどこの映画を見る。　or　映画より音楽の方が好きだけどこの映画を見る。
このテレビが前のテレビより大きい[です]！　or　前のテレビよりこのテレビの方が大きい[です]。
彼が大統領より有名だ。　or　大統領より彼の方が有名だ。

それに、それとも、そして、それで

よいと、わるいと、負けると、知ると、死ぬと、待つと、会うと、信じると、だと、ですと、くると、行くと、若いと

だろう、でしょう、でしょう

友達に誕生日のカードをあげた。　この古い本をくれませんか。　古い本をあげるよ。
最近上司から支持をいただいた。　彼女が学校で男の子からラブレターをもらった。

願いを叶えてあげる。　部下にレポートを書いてもらう。
日本語を教えてくれませんか。　部長が彼女に推薦状を書いていただいた。

毎朝、毎週、毎回

(The following are not the only possible combinations.)
彼女をデートに誘ったり、ロマンチックな散歩をしたり、素敵な一晩を過ごしたりした。
[I] invited her out on a date, [we] went on a romantic stroll, and we had a wonderful night.
早起きをしたり、コーヒーを買う余裕はなかったり、電車が遅れたりして最悪だった。
[I] woke up early, didn't have time to buy coffee, the train was late –it was aweful!
疲れて家に帰ってテレビを見たりした。
[I] was tired, [I] went home and [I] watched TV.
出かける準備をして駅で待ち合わせして友達と会ったり、映画館で映画を見たり楽しめた。
[I] prepared to go out, meet up at the station, ran into friend(s), watched a movie at the theater, and enjoyed [myself].

Chapter 14

(The following are not the only possible combinations.)
彼女をデートに誘ったし、ロマンチックな散歩をしたし、素敵な一晩を過ごした。
[I] invited her out on a date, [we] went on a romantic stroll, and we had a wonderful night.
早起きをしたし、コーヒーを買う余裕はなかったし、電車が遅れたし、最悪だった。
[I] woke up early, didn't have time to buy coffee, the train was late –it was aweful!
疲れたし、家に帰ったし、テレビを見た。
[I] was tired, [I] went home and [I] watched TV.
出かける準備をして駅で待ち合わせしたし、友達と会ったし、、映画館で映画を見たし、楽しめた。
[I] prepared to go out, meet up at the station, ran into friend(s), watched a movie at the theater, and enjoyed [myself].

Merges: 持って行く、歩いて帰る、解けていく、食べてみる、返してもらう

早く帰って寝るつもりだ。　来年に日本に行くから日本語を勉強するつもりだ。
飛行機に間に合わなかったのにスペインに行くつもりだ。

Is Saturday ok for [our] date? Sorry, [I] am a little busy on Saturday, but [I] am not very busy on Sunday. Because [I] don't drink alcoholic beverages all that much, is a café ok [for the meeting place]?

春休みを楽しみにしている。　草薙さんは3週間に休みを取っていないから今週末を楽しみにしているのだろう。　このデートを楽しみにしていましたか。

まーまー、まま、ママ、まーまー、まま、ママ、まま、ママ

この携帯はGPSが付いているのはとても便利だ。
The fact that this cell phone has GPS is very handy.
彼女がいつも遅いのが嫌いだ。
[I] hate the fact that she is always late.

知ること idea of knowing, knowledge, an idea/thing to be known
歩くこと idea of walking
帰ること idea of returning home
待つこと idea of waiting
見ること idea of seeing, something to be seen, something one has seen
生きること idea of living, what it means to live
死ぬこと idea of dying, what it means to die
買うこと idea of buying
売ること idea of selling
登ること idea of climbing

[Mr./Mrs.] Watanabe's goal is to know everything.   Going (the idea of going) to a foreign country while not understanding the language is stressful eh?   Learning a foreign language is an admirable thing, I think.

It's no good! I do not understand (know) what [I] should do!
[I] want to know if she likes me.
[I] will ask him if the report is already done or if it is not yet done.

Because there are many people who want to buy [it] the price will continue to rise.
Because [I/he/she/they] studied Japanese every day, [I/he/she/they] have come to understand Japanese.
[I] hated classical music when I was a kid, but, perhaps, [I] will go on to like [it].

Chapter 15

設定しておく、覚えておく、勉強しておく、決めておく、任せておく、送っておく

勉強しなければならない、帰らなければならない、行かなければならない、相談しなければならない
払わなければならない、飲まなければならない

(The following are not the only possible combinations.)
海外旅行の準備をしながら天気予報を聞く。
デザートを食べながら宿題について友達と話す。
テレビを見ながら勉強する。

(mainly C with a little M), M, M, (mainly C with a little M), M, C

It is about Brian's birthday party. It is about the 11 o'clock meeting.

いかせる、いかれる、いかされる
かえらせる、かえられる、かえらされる
はなさせる、はなされる、はなさせられる
わからせる、わかられる、わからされる
おもわせる、おもわれる、おもわされる
たべさせる、たべられる、たべされる
かたせる、かたれる、かたされる
かかせる、かかれる、かかされる
のませる、のまれる、のまされる
きえさせる、きえられる、きえされる
まけさせる、まけられる、まけされる
しなせる、しなれる、しなされる
いきさせる、いきられる、いきされる (use the alternate form: いかせる、いかれる、いかされる)
あそばせる、あそばれる、あそばされる
およがせる、およがれる、およがされる
こさせる、こられる、こされる
させる、される、させられる
あわせる、あわれる、あわされる

いって、いってください、いきなさい
かえって、かえってください、かえりなさい
はなして、はなしてください、はなしなさい
わかって、わかってください、わかりなさい
おもって、おもってください、おもいなさい
たべて、たべてください、たべなさい
かって、かってください、かちなさい
かいて、かいてください、かきなさい
のんで、のんでください、のみなさい
きえて、きえてください、きえなさい
まけて、まけてください、まけなさい

しんで、しんでください、しになさい
いきて、いきてください、いきなさい
あそんで、あそんでください、あそびなさい
およいで、およいでください、およぎなさい
きて、きてください、きなさい
して、してください、しなさい
あって、あってください、あいなさい

びしょびしょ、たまたま、ぐずぐず、ばたばた、ザーザー、ぺらぺら

いき、いきかた、　way of going, route, method of transport
かえり、かえりかた、　way of returning home, route, method of transport home
はなし、はなしかた、　way of conversing, tone, etc.
わかり、わかりかた、　way of understanding
おもい、おもいかた、　way of thinking/feeling
たべ、たべかた、　way of eating
かち、かちかた、　way of winning
かき、かきかた、　way of writing, one's handwriting
のみ、のみかた、　way of drinking
きえ、きえかた、　way of disappearing
まけ、まけかた、　way of losing
しに、しにかた、　way of dying
いき、いきかた、　way of living
あそび、あそびかた、　way of having fun
およぎ、およぎかた、　way of swimming
き、きかた、　way of coming, route, method of transport
し、しかた、　way of doing
あい、あいかた、　way of meeting

内、間に、間、内に

Chapter 16

彼はハンサムなので友達がたくさんいる。
あさみちゃんの成績はいいのにちゃんと毎日授業に来ない。
この車は世界中で一番早いので負けたことはない。
先生、患者がおきましたのに調子が悪くなっています。
松本さんは料理がうまい人なのでなんでも作れる。
新しい車を買いたいのにそんなに金がない。
二階建ての家なのにあまり広く感じない。
学校まで行ったのに宿題を忘れてしまった。

(these are not the only options)フロスティング、このかっこう(look/outfit)、二人、白、上田さん

パーティーに行くかどうかは知らない。
電車が4時半に来るかどうかは知りません。
映画が7時までに終わるかどうかを調べておく。

彼女がすしを食べたことがないから好きかどうかは分かりません。
仕事を辞めるかどうかはまだ決めていません。

旅行に行けるように貯金をする。
試験に合格するように彼女が三日間に勉強しました。
山口さんはドイツ語を勉強するようにドイツに行きます。
日本語を学ぶように勉強する。
プロジェクトを成功させるように協力してくれないと彼が言った。

掛かってある、食べている、飾ってある、書いております、覚えております、遅れている、つけてある

はずです、はずではない、はずではありません、はずだ、はずだ

なんでも、ここでも、どれでも、いつでも、だれでも

なにか、いつも、どこか、だれも、なぜか

言う、と言う、言っていない、という、という

かもしれない、かも、かもしれません、かもしれない

Made in the USA
San Bernardino, CA
16 June 2016